EXCEPTIONAL CREATURES

Stories from the Veterinary Field

Cat Whitney

ISBN: 149215329X
ISBN 13: 9781492153290

"A machine makes breaths as a machine makes buttons, all the same, but every breath of a creature is a creature itself, like no other, inestimably precious."
—Wendell Berry, *The Art of the Commonplace*

DEDICATION

If you're in here and you know it clap your hands!
If you're in here and you know it clap your hands!
If you're in here and you know it and you really want to show it,
If you're in here and you know it clap your hands!

PREFACE

Our relationships with animals, whether companion pets, food animals, wildlife or anything in between, function as an x-ray pointed at our psychology and our collective culture. The beam moves through the animal and out the other side. The resultant image is of things internal, illnesses and triumphs that were secret, old fractures and light areas that used to be dark. We used to be rural creatures, feeding chickens, sewing sealskin, riding horses and mushing dogs; we are hardwired to connect with other vertebrates. Yet looking closely means we stumble on revelations that are difficult. Americans spent over $53 billion on their pets in 2012, including food, sweaters and raincoats, veterinary care and heated pet beds. In 2012, primarily in areas far distant from average Americans, more than 55,000 people in our world died from the bites of unvaccinated rabid dogs. We have a vaccine for those dogs; it didn't get to them. We can be infantile, needy creatures when it comes to animals, ascribing human emotional traits. We use animals to feel heroic and self-righteous, to meet our needs to give and receive nurturance. At the same time, the presence of an animal in our lives is capable of cracking into suppressed, precious, human emotions that draw us closer to one another. They are a 'neutral love object' devoid of messy ambiguity and familial baggage.

What feels like a long time ago, I did formal training to become a veterinary technician, one of the best decisions I ever made. Becoming a licensed vet tech gave me geographic and financial flexibility, camaraderie, and a sense of accomplishment at an age when I needed it most. Wages as a vet tech have never been fabulous, but neither is the student loan debt students carry after earning a DVM degree. I've been able to work with countless species, in countless situations that I never would have anticipated. I haven't continued my work in the veterinary field because I love animals, however. My dirty little secret is that I work in the veterinary field because I love people. We are not dogs or cats or rabbits or horses or cattle or fish. We've manipulated a complex sociopolitical world in which to live, a world that alternately determines our lives and inspires us to change. We humans are the animals who kill each other for ideologies and resist food to prove a political point. We are exceptional creatures—unusual, uncommon, abnormal, atypical, extraordinary, rare, unprecedented, unexpected, surprising creatures—each and every one of us.

Writing about animals in modern America is traipsing through a social minefield. Very little incites more passion and outrage than the treatment and perception of animals. There seems to be no greater inter-organizational warfare than between animal rescue groups in the same community. Even when I lived in New Zealand, I watched factions within the SPCA sign petitions and boycotts regarding how to manage their animal population. If I state that dogs don't mind being neutered, or that killing puppies is OK, I fully expect vociferous objections from humans. On top of this, I have also entered the potentially explosive genre of memoir where readers will be outraged if it isn't perfectly true, but if I label the volume "fiction" they will be equally outraged because it *is* true. Our memories do often fail us, or the memories themselves manipulate us into compressing several different events, or we remember a person with specific details that answer our subconscious needs. Every story in this volume is "mostly true". There are some stories that I will levy are 99% accurate to the reality that occurred. One or two may rank as low as 60%. I even considered prefacing each chapter with clarification regarding these details, but these are not case histories in a medical journal.

We take the x-ray for the process of revelation, but the x-ray itself does not speak. We read an x-ray and interpret it for ourselves. Our knowledge, bias, training and feelings inform what we read in the image. Sometimes we have to go back again and again to re-vision and look with more insight. If I have done my job well, the one inarguable fact of this book is that the stories have been written with gratitude and great affection.

CONTENTS

1

CONDUCTIVITY

It is a little known fact that people working in the veterinary profession eat better and more often than even those in the restaurant industry. If you clear up a dog's yeast infection the owners will bring you cookies. Take out infected anal glands and you'll get banana bread. Head trauma, pancreatitis, urinary blockage and kennel cough can yield anything from fudge to cheese platters, depending on the season. I worked at one clinic where the owner purchased a new upright freezer just for all the Christmas treats, rationing them out so that we'd be dipping into Rudolph tins in July. Another practice allocated one whole gurney for edibles. On the sly, we used to take the truffles and set them up for fecal analysis in the lab.

Carletta Freemont made cheese Danishes. Carletta had a miniature schnauzer named Levi, an affable busy little dog always impeccably groomed and dressed. In his prime he was silver-gray with white fluffy eyebrows and beard, reminding me of a Dickens' character but without a limp or a wooden leg. Except for the hottest days in summer, Levi would always arrive in our clinic smartly outfitted in anything from a down jacket to a yellow raincoat. Carletta herself was somewhere between fifty and seventy years old. She deliberately worked at maintaining the mystery of her age. Her make-up was fastidiously applied, never overdone, her lip color always coordinated with her brown eyes and her hair. She had three wigs, one each in 'marigold', 'oak', and 'red salsa pearl' all in the same bouffant style, one that most of us envied for its lift and overall shine. Carletta spoke readily about her wigs when people complimented her hair "Oh, you are so sweet! You like this one, honey? First time I've had it on in weeks! Spring is almost here—*Praise Jesus*—and it's time for change!"

I'd survived three decades of living before ever meeting anyone who actually made cheese Danishes, so I almost thought that the Bible verses Carletta wrote on business cards and affixed to the bottom of each pastry where a type of tradition, the way finding an almond in the rice pudding wins you a marzipan pig or something. The cards were hand written. The quotes were very often about food, manna, breaking bread, sustenance from the Lord. No one ever opened their mouth and read one aloud, the way you do with fortune cookies. Instead, we all read them in solemn earnest, sometimes hiding them in our pockets, more often watching them collect in one drawer in the break room that held extra ketchup and soy sauce packets, as if we might need them in the future.

The hard truth of Levi's entrance into Carletta's life was that her daughter left him to her after she committed suicide. No one spoke of this; we knew it the way we knew about Carletta's Danishes, the reality was so attached to her that it'd become as invisible as air.

Levi was nine months old when he came under Carletta's care. Over the years he visited us for his vaccinations, nail trims, a scare with a ham bone, one exploratory surgery because he ate a sponge, and his annual dose of tranquilizers to prepare for July 4th fireworks.

At age six Levi developed diabetes. This doesn't have to be a big deal in dogs, if you catch it early. Attentive as ever, Carletta knew right away. I was the one who took her call "Sweetie, I think we better schedule an appointment, Levi drinks his bowl desert-dry and he's pissing rivers all over my kitchen floor!"

"You're right, that sure doesn't sound like him. How long has this been going on?"

"Sweetie, I don't know but he wakes me up in the middle of the night with the sound of that stream on that linoleum, a real gusher, like my late husband after his prostate problems—loud and proud. But Levi isn't proud, of course, you know how they get that ashamed look on their face."

It wasn't a question. I made a grunting noise. I scheduled her for later that day and she finished, the way she always ended a call, "May God bless your day."

When Levi came in we tested his blood and urine, confirmed diabetes, and kept him for another day in the hospital while we repeatedly poked his neck and legs to either draw blood or inject insulin. The little fellow took it all with great aplomb while we, with simmering, silent, hedonistic glee, fixed our minds on when the Danishes would arrive.

Levi did a beautiful job of being diabetic for almost three years. Carletta brought him in for every recheck appointment and blood draw, in addition to his nail trims, occasional ear cleanings and to return full baggies of used insulin syringes. We never had to change his insulin dose; he motored right along on the same three units just fine. He got a little grayer around the muzzle and developed a faint white ridge along his back—like a miniature silverback gorilla, but otherwise maintained his poise.

Then came a day in early March when something was not right. Carletta called. She described Levi as "one brick short of a wall". Someone else took the call, a co-worker I knew well enough to discern, from the timbre of her voice and the slouch of her shoulders, that this might not be a simple thing.

When I came up to the lobby to greet them and escort Levi back for some diagnostic work, I saw Carletta before she saw me. She was staring at the coffee service, at the pillar of Styrofoam cups stacked much higher than normal. Her face was pensive. For once it seemed that her wig was a little lopsided. Then she saw me and put back on her public face. "Hi honey! I think Levi needs an oil change and tune-up, he vomits whatever I give him, and I can imagine that's he's over sweetened with his sugar."

"Great to see you! Yeah, you did the right thing bringing him in. We'll take care of him." I used my deepest 'we've seen everything and have treatments for it all' voice. I brought them both into an exam room and took Levi back for blood and urine tests as well as an x-ray.

Sometimes you can tell just by looking at an animal. It's simple pattern recognition. After you have seen hundreds of dogs in renal failure you take the leash from an owner and you just get a feeling. Perhaps it is a slight tilt to the head, a change in gait. Up close it could be the smell of the breath or color of the sclera of the eyes. Levi wasn't acting horribly ill, but the first signs of kidney failure, as he was showing, don't begin until 75% of kidney function was gone. If we could support the remaining 25% of functional nephrons, while not skewing his diabetes too badly, we could buy him some more quality time.

We kept Levi in the hospital for two days on intravenous fluids to flush out the toxins in his blood that were making him vomit. He was depressed in his little stainless steel hospital cage. Carletta came every day and sat back in the hospital treatment area on an upturned garbage can looking into his cage. She was so enraptured, sitting there, that whatever we were doing behind her failed to startle her in the slightest. Soft prayers flowed between Levi and Carletta.

By day three his blood kidney values were enormously improved and he was eating. We sent him home with Carletta, for the first time hoping that she would *not* make us Danishes. There were no happy endings for the type of renal failure Levi had, and despite all her efforts to get her makeup and outfits perfect, small stress fractures in her appearance and grooming had begun to appear. One fingernail chipped. Two strands of white hair peeking out from under the wig. A slur of mascara on her upper cheek. But, she made Danishes. She had a recheck for Levi scheduled one week later.

I always reflect on Levi and Carletta set to the backdrop of spring. April, in the northern town I was living in, was the time of snowmelt.

Depending on how much snow we'd been graced with, it was also a time of enormous inconvenience. Mud stymied unpaved roads. Ice and snow on roofs cracked and slid off in tectonic sheets, sometimes taking off chimneys, sometimes gravely injuring people and pets. Closer to the city center pedestrians would get drenched by the upsurge of runoff under the wheels of passing cars. And basement after basement flooded. Our clinic was no different that spring. I spent an entire afternoon in the basement lifting boxes of overstock bandage material from certain doom on the floor onto wire shelves. Our flooding happened gradually, but it took more than a week and four service men to figure out the trouble and stop the waters from rising. It was during this time that Levi and Carletta came in for their recheck appointment.

A key component in managing renal failure in pets is keeping an eye on their blood pressure. In an awake animal (one not under anesthesia for a surgery) this is easier said than done. Animals are furry. You have to shave a small spot to have skin access to vessels. Cats awake in a veterinary hospital, amidst barking dogs, are the least agreeable patients for this. Dogs hate having their feet or tails touched, the most common places from which to read pressure. We use the same kind of cuff and squeezy device (called a sphygmomanometer) used in human medicine, but instead of a stethoscope we use an ultrasonic Doppler crystal to hear the blood flow in the pet. The Parks Doppler is a tedious device. The sensitive crystal is housed inside a square casing the size of your pinky fingernail, which is attached to a cord that runs to a sound box with two dials. Once you go through the machinations of shaving the pet's paw, you mound the tiny crystal with ultrasound gel and attempt to tape it to your patient. While trying to keep the crystal in place, you turn on the Doppler and are bombarded with what acoustically amounts to 'snow' on a TV screen. It's like having someone rub Brillo on your eardrum. You then adjust the dials, simultaneously adjusting the placement of the crystal on the pet, until you hear the wave-like rushing of the animal's blood. It can be thrilling to finally hear it, that audible testament to the body's machinery at work, its aliveness. It can also be thrilling because you just spent one full hour trying to find it.

Levi sat on the treatment table placidly. His vigor from a month ago was replaced with a resignation. That peculiar odor of a kidney patient was back. I placed the Doppler as I always did while one of my co-workers had a hand on his back. I put my ear close to the microphone clicked on the sound to lowest volume. At first, all I heard was the familiar hiss and sizzle of indeterminate sound waves. I took a few seconds to minutely shift the crystal on Levi's paw, all the time listening for the wave-sound of his blood. Then I heard something that I had never, ever heard before, very quietly at first, then much, much louder as I turned the Doppler speaker up. ". . AND WHEN YOOOU COME TO JESUS BROTHERS AND SISTERS . . .". The cadence and delivery of a charismatic sermon is unmistakable, words crashing up and down like a bellowed fire, a powerful tremor to the timbre of the words." . . . WHEN YOOOU COME TO JESUS AND YOU LET THAT SPRING RAIN WAAASH . . .".

I looked up from Levi and the Doppler. Two doctors, three technicians, one assistant, and a receptionist holding a file she was about to hand off stood stock still, mouths agape. Someone finally broke the silence. "Well, they ARE sound waves." She was referring to radio waves, the only plausible explanation for what seemed to be coming from Levi. Someone else, "Do you think it's coming from across the street?" Behind the gas station and convenience store next door was a "worship center" but none of us had ever been inside. Levi's primary doctor looked at me and said, with no amusement, "You better go get Carletta".

Up in the waiting area Carletta was sitting in a shaft of sunlight looking far away. "Carletta?" When she turned her face I could see the dark circles around her eyes. It occurred to me that I honestly did not know if she had any remaining family.

"Levi's doing fine, but I think you need to hear what we picked up while taking his blood pressure."

We walked back to the treatment area, Carletta somehow picking up on my awe and expectancy.

One of the veterinarians had turned the volume up on the Doppler and, amidst the crackles and fuzzy radio sounds, the preacher's voice rolled forth "…AAAND ON THAT DAY THE LORD'S HAND WILL REACH, REACH FOR HIS CHILDREN AND GATHER THEM TO HIS BOSOM . . .".

I quickly slid a chair under Carletta; none of us wanted to see her fall to her knees on the treatment room floor. She looked up at the girl still scratching the lower back of Levi, though he clearly did not need someone to hold him still. Carletta's mouth was a perfect "o". She gently slid her fingers up the slim cable that attached the talking box to her little dog, searching for the source of the miracle. Levi sat like a gray stone tableau, as if he were conscious of the words emanating from inside him, and their import. " . . . AND READY OURSELVES FOR DELIVERY UNTO HIS GRACE WE . . .".

It was a few more minutes before I noticed the tears dripping off Carletta's chin. She was not blinking, nor making any other expression, but wide, wet tears trailed her cheeks, drawing mascara with them. None of us wanted to interrupt them. Where they there for fifteen minutes? Thirty-minutes? Those of us still working in the back were quieter than we'd ever been before. Even the mastiff dog who came back for a nail trim seemed to subdued once he entered the sphere of Carletta and Levi's influence. At some point, however, Carletta rose to leave and we took the Doppler crystal off Levi.

The story with Levi does not go on much longer after this. Veterinary medicine diverges from human medicine at one special point: we have the power to end suffering, and to end life. Often this is a great, great burden as we try and help clients make the right decision at the right time for both themselves and their pet. No one is prepared to play God. Those that think they are have no business doing so.

Carletta moved through the last two weeks of Levi's life with a level of composure and dignity we rarely see. Every time we adjusted his medication or had him come in for subcutaneous fluids she would ask just enough questions to take care of business, but never enter into the frantic quality-of-life-how-much-will-this-cost discussion that so burdened most people. When Levi began vomiting up even water, after she'd begun to have to carry him outside to urinate and defecate, she called up and only said "I think it's time". And so it was. By the time the little creature came in he was skin and bones, his silver fur a dull gray, the whites of his eyes and membranes of his mouth a mustard color. It was difficult to even find a vessel in which to inject the pentobarbital, but we did. Carletta was talking to him the whole time, stroking the top of his head then whispering into his ear. I like to imagine Levi, on the other side of our injection, bounding towards the bright, bright light.

One, two, then three days went by without Danishes from Carletta. But on day four she dropped off a double batch. Each one had the requisite scripture quote, focusing on joy, release, union with one's creator. We didn't empty the platter of treats until the second day, leaving only crumbs and a smear of frosting. But when someone lifted up the platter to take it to kitchen they noticed something. A 4x6 photo was taped to the bottom of the platter. A young woman, with auburn hair and green eyes, in a red sweater and pearls, sat in an overstuffed armchair. The branches of a Christmas tree intruded into the photo from the left. The young woman had a broad smile that reached to the corner of her eyes. In her arms was a small, silver, schnauzer puppy.

2

BABY REEFER

I don't know who did the counting, but there are approximately 220 million domestic cats in the world. It amazes me that, within this global milieu of fur and claws, that the right cats always find the right owners. Once, just after we euthanized an elderly cat of a trusted client who'd managed to keep her sense of humor throughout her pet's long illness, the owner looked up at us with a smile and said, "The cat gods will know there is an opening at my house. Hopefully they won't send more than one, like they did last time when Queenie found me with a belly full of kittens." The veterinarian and I were still laughing when we returned to the treatment area. "What kind of euthanasia was *that?*" someone asked.

Cats are the only species of carnivore that has allowed themselves to be domesticated by man. And they are fertile. The pineal gland in cats keeps its inward eye on the length of daylight hours, signaling the estrous cycle when things tip past the vernal equinox. This means that all the cats begin to go on their dates in spring and 63 days later, the kittens arrive. Veterinary clinics and shelters easily become overwhelmed during "kitten season". We see litters of kittens come in cardboard beer boxes, Easter baskets, wrapped in towels, in Tupperware, caught in fly paper. (We had a Jiffy Lube employee bring in a tiny kitten he found when he opened a car hood at work. It didn't belong to the car's owner. The young employee kept the cat and called him Pennzoil.) And, because these tiny creatures are so small and curious they are easily damaged: shut in car doors, stepped on, left in the refrigerator's crisper drawer overnight, folded into the hide-a-bed. Terrible illnesses also befall young kittens, but for all their fragility, their resiliency reigns.

It was late August when he came into the hospital in a shoebox. Clutching the shoebox was a young woman with red, moist eyes, "But he was totally fine yesterday!" She extended the box with a tremulous hand. I looked inside. On top of a cloth napkin was a miniature orange tabby with stripes like those on dollhouse curtains, a nose like an eraser head. He was a blotched tabby, one whose stripes spiral at the midsection instead of running vertically, and he had white paws in the front and a white bib. But this kitten was not moving. At all.

"What's wrong with him?" The woman pleaded.

"Let me take him in the back and get a temperature while Dana finishes checking you in."

This hospital was much larger than some of the others I'd worked in. The treatment area was not a cloistered, congested area of chaotic events, people sitting on dogs to trim their nails or draw blood, overturned pill vials from moving too fast, someone cursing at the label printer. The treatment area in this clinic had wide, white, vaulted ceilings, a separate area for dental procedures, and even two human-infant incubators in the surgery area to warm chilled patients. One of my all-time favorite doctors was working that day. Dr. Krystal Doran came over when she saw me pull the orange ball of fur from the box. He hung from my hand like a wet sock "What's this?" She asked.

"This is your 4:30."

"You're shitting me . . . this is an appointment?" What Doran meant was that this was an emergency. She immediately pulled out her stethoscope and placed in on the tiny ribcage. The bell of the stethoscope almost covered the whole kitten. I looked at her. Her face was furrowed in confusion.

"His heart rate is 140. Strong." She said. Kittens in action have heart rates too high to count, but Doran had expected a heart rate indicative of imminent death.

I touched the corner of his eyes. His blink reflex worked fine. His temperature was 99.5°F, a little low but not alarmingly so. Doran took out a pair of hemostats to check for a deep pain response, a barometer for nervous system functioning. She pinched a tiny toe with the instrument and—yup-—the foot pulled back lickety-split. "What does he weigh?" Doran asked.

I had not yet weighed the little animal. I went and got the smallest scale we had. One-pound-two-ounces. That would make him about seven weeks old. Two pounds typically equaled a kitten that was eight weeks of age.

"His color is good." I said. When I opened his mouth it was pink as Bazooka gum, a flicker of tongue letting go from the way it stuck to his hard palate and falling back against teeth the size of grains of rice.

"Well fuck, I'm stumped." She hit the last syllable of her words so hard that a drop of spit arched from her lips.

Doran wore nail polish and the occasional ankle-length skirt and had talents in explaining viral replication to a clients, but she added the vigor and vocabulary of of an auto mechanic to the place. An older and bolder technician joked with her all the time about being "trailer trash", about how she made recipes with cans of Veg-All and salads with colored marshmallows. She was in her mid-forties, had freckles under her bright green eyes, a comfortable slouch to her silhouette, and meaty legs that did not taper at knee and ankle. She had strong forearms, usually wearing a bracelet with Christian insignia. Her upper arms were soft. She cried easily and often. There was a day when someone accidentally scheduled three dog euthanasias back-to-back and immediately afterwards she went into the x-ray room, locked the door, and wept with loud, gasping, snotty gulps. Dr. Doran was the veterinarian who would take patients home for care, who would call owners after business hours to share information. She served veterinary medicine home-style. But, taking the good with the bad, I can say she often overscheduled herself, being forced to simply hoard patients in the back treatment area for radiographs or other treatments we couldn't perform until after closing. She forgot things. One day she forgot she had an appointment waiting for her and she went to lunch. For an hour-and-a-half. Another time, after working a 10-hour Saturday, during which time someone dropped off a seagull with an alleged broken wing, it was her idea to walk out to the parking lot to "see if it could fly". It couldn't. But it could run! We ended up running more than half-a-block in the evening dusk before it lodged itself in a shrub where we could grab it. But Doran's compassion simply didn't burn out. Her boundary between personal and professional was fluid.

After her expletive, Doran looked down at the kitten again, putting her thumb between his small ears in a quick stroke of affection before turning to go speak with the owner.

The kitten was just cold enough to need heat support but our incubators were all in use. One had a dachshund dying of kidney failure in it, the other a thirty-pound fuzzy white dog wedged in like a Christmas turkey. He'd just had a dental with some teeth extractions and he bobbed his head from side-to-side like Stevie Wonder because of the ketamine anesthetic. Every time he did so he smeared bloody drool on the inside of the Plexiglas. Damn, I thought, I hate taking those things apart to clean them. Instead I did what we do to warm newborns and hamsters. I filled a broad-brimmed bowl with warm water, floated a trash bag on top and let the tiny animal ride on a waterbed.

Doran came back through the door, her face pinched. "There's no money". This is often the death knell for a patient. It is impossible to meet the demands for free or reduced cost services and not have all the employees in the clinic living in cardboard boxes with wages under $3.00 per hour. It's a common misunderstanding that we overcharge. What we do not have is the backbone of the insurance industry (yet). We use the same equipment and supplies as human medicine but receive no discount on their purchase. All of this means nothing, of course, if it is you faced with the very difficult choices.

"I asked her if she'd like to sign him over." Doran said.

My chin jerked up to look at her. It meant the kitten would become property of the clinic, we would incur all costs of treatment, and the office manager would shit pink Twinkies. Doran knew this. She also knew that, if we succeeded in bringing the little guy back from the dead, the onus of adopting him out would be on our shoulders, too. In the summer season of plentiful kittens this wasn't always easy. Everyone was aware of that challenge at this time of year, the contradiction between the pleasure of admiring and working with baby cats and the reality that such a precious commodity was cheap and plentiful.

"Well,—" Doran said, looking down at the little orange body floating in the bed I'd made. "What would you do?" Another fine Doran quality: truly valuing the input of her technicians.

She was right, except for being in some kind of coma, the kitten was perfectly healthy.

"Any ideas at all about what's wrong?" I ventured.

"I asked Dana to call for his records. The owner said she went to that new clinic on 32nd yesterday."

As if on queue, Dana pushed through the doors with the faxed paperwork. It was a modern clinic, but with a very old fax machine that reproduced any handwritten record with unreadable grittiness. Doran saw it before I did. She elongated the syllables as if in a fatalistic sigh, "Ooooh, craaaP". Then I saw it, too. This kitten had been given injectable ivermectin for ear mites.

Ivermectin is a medication that looks like clear corn syrup. For an 800-pound cow a mere tablespoon of the stuff (injected under the skin) will rid the poor beast of everything from tapeworms to lice. In a sheep that weighs 150 pounds you need half a teaspoon to get the same effect. The medication vanquishes almost any parasite within 24 hours, leaving farmers to gaze with satisfaction at excrement littered with the pieces and parts of dead hangers-on (or in). It can be used to treat ear mites in cats and dogs; the problem is measuring the proper volume for an animal that is not a cow. In this case, even when they used a tuberculin syringe, the kitten was given more than ten times the correct dose.

Without saying anything more, Doran turned and went back to speak to the owner.

The owner relinquished the kitten, asking only to be notified if he died. We put a hair-thin catheter in one of his legs and ran some fluids into him. We dedicated one of our incubators to his care, where we had to tape his intravenous fluid line along the edge to avoid having the weight of it drag his small body to the edge, like he was caught on the end of a fishing line and were being reeled in. Every four hours we turned his tiny body over, as if he were an English muffin that needed toasting on both sides. Once or twice we tried to feed him with food from a syringe, stroking his throat to elicit a swallow. This went on for three days. There was enough work and other patients to worry about that I was able to divorce myself from the outcome; you do learn to numb-out after a while. The Doran trait that I admired most, however, was her ability to stay open and never, ever, run out of hope.

I was the morning opener for the clinic at that time, arriving at 6:30. There's something intimate about being alone inside any building that is normally a hive of activity, buildings like schools, restaurants, and churches. It feels as if the whole building is sighing an airy, ghostly breath after the burden of containing life's dramas, or as if it is a lover just waiting for the next torrid affair. Veterinary clinics are no different. I came in that morning as I usually did. I disarmed the alarm system, turned on the light, and began to hit buttons to wake up the computers. I listened to my own footfall as I went up the stairs to hang my coat and leave my lunch in the refrigerator. Returning downstairs, I realized that something was beeping. The wall-mounted air freshener? It did that when its air canister of 'ocean breeze' was empty. Then I checked the battery back up we used during power outages—still no. It was coming from the treatment area. I switched the hallway lights on and went back.

The beeping was coming from the machine delivering the kitten's fluid. But the fluid line was not attached to the kitten. Instead, the tiny animal was pacing the cage like a starved lion, bawling an open-mouthed squeak with every step. He'd pulled the catheter out of his vein overnight. I practically ran to the food cupboard, grabbing several cans of different flavors in case he needed coaxing to eat. I pulled the pop-top on the 'ocean whitefish' flavor and as soon as I cracked the lid to the incubator, he pushed himself out and towards the food so fast that he fell on the floor before I could catch him. Fortunately, young kittens have a lot of cartilage where their joints should be, their bones haven't fully calcified, so they have just a little "bounce" to them. I picked him up and watched him thrust his face into the can of food, making a low growl while working away. I was exhilarated, smitten, triumphant, and in love with the providence of the universe, all at the same time. I ran to the phone to call Doran, forgetting that she was not a morning person.

"Hellow?" She sounded like there was a wet rag in her mouth.

"He's up! He's up and he's eating!"

"Who's up?" She sounded a little more interested.

"The *kitten!*" The tone of my voice tacitly added the word stupid to the end of my exclamation.

"Seriously! That's awesome!" She was certainly awake then. I could almost hear her feet hitting the floor as she sat up on her bed. "I'll be in by 8 a.m." I knew this actually meant nine.

Once Doran came in she did another exam on the kitten and his vital signs were perfectly normal. We took him out of the incubator and set him up in a cage,

As our day came to a close, Doran decided that, just to be on the safe side, she'd take the kitten home for observation overnight. She was down to only one old golden retriever and an iguana, having lost her one-eyed diabetic cat a few months ago and her Doberman a year before. We put the frenzied little fellow in a carrier and put a leaning tower of cat food cans in a bag.

The following morning began without incident. When Doran arrived around 9 she dropped the cat carrier in the treatment area for us before she went up to her office to look at her schedule for the day. The kitten was howling to be let out, practically rattling his bars. I'd left his cage set up from the day before, and I glibly plucked him from his crate. Then it hit me.

He smelled. And he bore the odor of one particular substance.

I knew that pungent sweetness, that dirty sock, dank basement warmth with a hint of toast and freshly cut lawn. "Shelby," I called to another technician tentatively, "I need you to smell this cat." Shelby came out from running a sample in the lab. "What?" She was walking towards me as she said it.

In my slow-motion memory, Shelby took several minutes to turn her face back up to mine after sniffing the kitten. Her eyes became enormous, her face at once glowing with disbelief, dismay, and hilarity. Then she made the pronouncement: "It's marijuana".

We called the kitten Baby Reefer from then on, even making a sign for his cage. We volleyed a thousand jokes about his appetite. Doran, of course, was mortified. The story we heard was that Baby Reefer was kept in her teenage son's room for the night. Adam was about seventeen and it was no secret that he'd begun to attend AA meetings after two DUI incidents. He had told her he was going to a meeting that night, but had come home around 2 a.m. Not feeling like a confrontation in the middle of the night, Doran had simply rolled over. Sometime between 2 and 7 a.m. Baby Reefer had acquired his name.

He stayed with us for the next few days, each of us taking turns bringing him up to the break room during our lunches to watch his antics and hear him thrum with purring when we grabbed him. We knew we couldn't have a resident clinic cat, but we sincerely wished.

All too soon, the cat gods had leaked our secret. A woman called our clinic looking to acquire an orange cat. Dana asked her enough questions to ascertain that it was not for a color-specific cult ritual or deviant purpose, but because her childhood cat was an orange tabby and, because her husband had been allergic, she'd been unable to have a cat ever since. "Well, we have an orange tabby cat," Dana began, then using the only dissuasive detail she could think of "but he's a very small cat."

The woman arrived later that day and was lead to the most comfortable exam room we had, the one with the leather chair and stool right next to the exam table. When I brought Baby Reefer into the room her hands fled to her mouth, her eyes softened, almost in tears. Then she reached for him as a child would for a stuffed bear. I left them there to go and get his favorite crinkle ball, the shiny one that sounded like crispy birthday wrap, and a bowl of water in case their visit lasted longer than a few minutes. When I returned Doran was perched on the stool watching the bonding with satisfaction.

Suddenly, without looking up from a laughable game of fetch with Reefer, the woman asked, "Have you guys named him yet?" I shot a look at Doran, who got off her stool stiffly. After a moment's pause she said, "We've been calling him Coral. Coral Reefer." My hand fled to my mouth and I had to turn to leave the room to prevent outright laughter.

"Oh that's a pretty name, very unusual," the woman answered. "Do you scuba dive?"

Doran answered in a dismissive tone "Once, in Hawaii. Very memorable."

Doran kept an earnest, straight face while I shakily excused myself.

When she finally came into the back treatment area we looked at each other and lost it completely. Doran was practically crying when she choked out "I . . . have . . . never . . . been scuba diving."

Within a few months I'd left that clinic to get an English degree and do some overseas travel. But the tides of fate always turn around and I found myself easily welcomed back into the very same clinic. Little had changed. Doran still practiced home-style medicine. Kitten season still rolled around every year. And, whenever I went up to the doctors' offices I looked up at the framed 8x10 of a majestic orange tabby poised on his haunches in front of a window, with a white bib, brilliant eyes, and something of a feline smile. He sat atop the words "With gratitude! Love, Maryanne and Coral".

interlude: Green Apple and Gruyere

There are male veterinary technicians just as there are male calico cats. They're rare, fascinating, endearing, and come with special adaptive traits. I met one fellow who was the father of two young children who taught me how to holler "Code Brown!" for diarrhea, "Code Green!" when it was payday, and "Code Jubilee!" when someone brought food . In my early years at the clinic with Doran a handsome twenty-two-year-old boy who was well over six feet tall broke into our women-only clinic. Five women veterinarians and enough support staff to total thirty-six female employees had left the owner on the EEO defensive, but along came Greg. He had a thick thatch of chest hair peaking out from his scrubs, where he used to snuggle neonate kittens to keep them warm. He'd ridden the rodeo circuit in the midwest, accruing awards and injuries that acted up at odd moments. I'd worked alongside him for several weeks when I finally asked, as we were waiting for our film radiographs to develop, "So, do you have kids? Are you married?" I became the last person in the building to be told, while he laughed good-naturedly, that he was very, very homosexual. Hadn't I noticed him ogling the roofers there last week? No, Greg, I had not.

Greg had maxed out his rodeo awards, passed his vet tech exam, and had his next accomplishment planned—culinary school. My last day at the clinic he made a lasagna with green apples and Gruyere cheese and stuck a few candles in it. We'd been on a streak of treating small dogs and cats under a few pounds, so when he passed me the lasagna to put on the gurney alongside paper plates I felt my whole body give way with the heft of the thing. I dared him to put it on the cat scale. *You do it. No, you . . ..*

When the lasagna finally made it to the cat scale it registered 12.5 pounds. Best damn thing I ever ate.

3

GOLDIE

I f you work in a small town veterinary clinic you get to know your animal control officers. They're always dressed up as if they're entering your clinic to diffuse a bomb, their bulletproof chest guards and badges announcing drama, their black pants with a fat radio in a holster that crackles with static and occasionally breaks into a voice . . . six-month-old lab on 20th and May street, DOA . . . kittens left in apartment on post after PCS orders . . . third report nuisance beaver at the housing complex off West Side slough . . . The most frequent officer at our clinic was Geoff, practical and firm, with a half-smile he used in place of a laugh.

Whenever Geoff came into the clinic we knew he had a story, and we'd all gather around him as if he were Santa. Sometimes it is a happy story, like a tiny kitten rescued from a drain pipe. Sometimes it's a sad story we can turn into happy. He once brought us a seven-month-old female pit bull puppy who'd been shot in the chest. A younger veterinarian did the surgery, named her "Guido" and brought her back-and-forth to work every day in a red duffle bag until she could get up and play.

One of Geoff's partners at Animal Control picked up Goldie in a grocery store parking lot after an employee reported a golden retriever sitting in front of the delivery entrance for two full days. Her red collar had her name engraved on a gold-bone tag, but there was no contact information on the other side. The reporting individual said she didn't really seem sick, but she was very, very thirsty and very, very tired.

"This is Goldie, I believe." Geoff said as he held out the leash to our young kennel girl. Sarah was sixteen. She walked over from her high school every afternoon with her work scrubs in a bag and fond hopes of becoming a veterinarian.

There were a few things to notice about Goldie right off. She had the endearing attentive personality that invented the epithet "man's best friend". Her caramel-colored golden retriever 'feathers' were caked in April mud and speckled with it higher up on her chest and abdomen, as if she'd been running beside the road, splashing through runoff, and then lying down in puddles like an elephant trying to cool off.

"There's a problem with her collar." Geoff leaned down and swept some of Goldie's soft neck fur away to reveal the red nylon. A communal nose-wrinkling of disgust and the sound "uuuuuugh" blew noxiously from our little circle in symphony. The collar must've been placed on Goldie when she was a small pup and then never adjusted for her growth. Like a sign nailed to a sapling and left to be covered by an overgrowth of tree bark, the body had tried to live with the foreign material imbedded into the flesh as best it could. The wound smelled like rotten shellfish. The good news was that we could turn that kind of problem completely around in just days.

"She has another problem, Geoff." Dr. Vance said, from a meditative distance. He stated it without surprise or dismay, and with neither despair nor resignation.

Dr. Harold Vance was about sixty when I worked for him. He was a little Scottish fellow, hair a reddish blond, maybe 5'9", a product of a 1960's veterinary education, a time of male camaraderie, when Vance and his classmates would put on Rodgers & Hammerstein musicals with all the words changed to be veterinary flash cards for the next exam. He would occasionally break into song during surgery, something to the tune of 'Oklahoma' that began *"Heme-a-tome-a! when the blood comes rushing from the veins . . . and the histamines . . ."* .

When Vance graduated from vet school, the entire nature of liability, insurance, the Drug Enforcement Agency, and the Department of Occupational Licensing had been different. Certainly he'd been counseled in the hazards of dispensing controlled, addictive substances to clients, but it was nothing like the hazing that the students of the 90's and 2000's had to endure. The new crop of vet students had been so felled by promises of litigation and the stripping of their veterinary license that some were afraid to let an owner hold her own pet for vaccination.

Our clinic was located in a town that functioned as a hub for other rural areas only accessible by plane. People would call from these villages with dogs covered in porcupine quills, fishhooks in their throats, or situations far more desperate. I have memories of putting the clients on hold and walking into Vance's office with their name on a piece of paper. He'd read the name, nod, then write down what I could send. I'd wrap those tiny, brown, precious bottles in paper and put them in their cardboard box. I suspect, for Vance, he was old enough to know that bad things happen, just usually not the things you were trying to insure against.

Another time I was tending a dog that was running a fever. Nothing was bringing the fever down, not ice packs, not alcohol sprayed on the paws, not antibiotics.

"Come with me" Vance said conspiratorily. I followed him into his office, a place with wood paneling, shag carpeting, a shiny red leather office chair and the sensation of walking into a glove. He opened his liquor cabinet under the window and pulled out a drug called Dipyrone. "Give 1 ml of this sub-Q. Then put it back in here. It's off the market; they don't make it anymore."

There were two other veterinarians in town from the same era, both a bit older. Dr Frye had just turned 90, and the town's veterinary community had to throw an informal retirement party to cue him to close his office. Though his desire to practice veterinary medicine hadn't ebbed, he'd begun to take cats in for neutering and hand them back with one remaining testicle. When I'd first met him he'd given me a hug instead of a handshake. It surprised me; it was unusual. But it was innocently honed on years of watching veterinary nurses pour out compassion and tears. In other small towns and in other countries I would meet elders exactly like him, a balustrade of old men along the edge of change.

There were two jokes Vance could not let go of. The first was that he was about to go into an appointment with a snake that had a reptile dysfunction. The second was that his favorite drink was made of Pabst Blue Ribbon beer and Smirnoff vodka: a "PabstSmir". Newly hired employees had trouble accepting Vance's sense of humor at face value. I was once helping a new girl prepare female pups for their spay procedure, something that involves expressing a full bladder to get it out of the way for surgery in the abdomen. Vance came over to see his surgery specimens and the new gal suddenly sent a jet of urine right into the crotch of Vance's trousers. He disappeared and came back in scrub bottoms, saying "You girls sure know how to get a man out of his pants!"

And then there was the very first state veterinary conference I attended. The food is never much to talk about at such things but there are cocktails. Dr. Vance had to make some announcements on behalf of the organization in our part of the state. He'd had a drink, or maybe a few. He walked up to the microphone and started the typical "CAN YOU HEAR ME?" We nodded and grunted our assent. Still, he said again "CAN YOU HEAR ME?" There was some snickering from his audience and then a louder version of confirmation. Those who'd known him for ten or twenty years knew this was the character they got when he'd imbibed a healthy number of scotch and sodas. Then Vance, still holding the microphone, opened the sliding glass door behind him, backed into the night and closed the door in front of him. We watched his exuberant mouth make the soundless words "CAN YOU HEAR ME NOW?" from his open-air theatre on the other side of the glass.

With Geoff there that day, and Sarah squatting in front of Goldie, squeezing clumps of mud into dust and sweeping them off her fur, we considered Vance's pronouncement. We stood there longer than normal, longer than it took to recognize what he was talking about because we needed to think about what it meant in her particular case.

"I'll set up x-ray" Zoe said. Zoe was a single mom of two boys and very active in the community rescuing and rehoming golden retrievers.

With bright eyes and tail held high Goldie tried to jump up on the x-ray table for us, but she was weighed down by the stone-like bulk of her belly. I pushed her rear while Zoe supported her front. Once on the table, she lay on her side, lightly panting, seeming to enjoy the flat coolness of being recumbent in a dimly lit room. She stretched her legs out, her midsection tall and round.

Our x-ray came out clear and shrill. I heard the shuffle of Vance's loafers coming around the corner. He looked at the x-ray and sighed deeply. With a black marker he began outlining the crown of each puppy skull in Goldie's abdomen. The larger breed dogs can have many pups at a time and you have to be careful not to get caught up in counting spines or tiny femurs or you won't get an accurate number. Even with the skull technique one or two little fellows always hide behind a loop of bowel. "I get eleven." Vance announced. "You girls can check me after we find her a kennel." He turned around and stroked Goldie's face, then squeezed one of her teats. A drop of milk beaded out.

Goldie was not just one homeless dog, she was an envelope of eleven homeless dogs, perhaps more.

To begin a discussion about stray animal management and pet overpopulation is fruitless. This is not an issue perpetuated by anonymous evil people, but nor will the average citizen stand up, raise their hands, and claim "I am part of the problem!" Animal shelters around the country are staffed by caring people who love animals. And these people are braced somewhere between public policy, funding, and human emotion. In our town, at that time, returning Goldie to the shelter meant one of two things—either a good Samaritan from one of the already-taxed foster programs would agree to feed, clean and house Goldie and family for three months, or she and her unborn would be euthanized at the shelter. Animal Control had a $200 spending limit on medical care with us for any animal.

If Goldie had an owner then a third option would be available: ovariohysterectomy, or "a spay". When we do this on an owner's animal we do it earlier than with Goldie. We do it before the pups are viable, when they are still shaped like chicken eggs inside a pouch. The owners pay; it's at least double the cost of a regular spay. It's a difficult surgery; we lament the loss, but we do it. We clamp off the artery at the cervix with huge clamps, we close the accessory vessels, and we remove the uterus. We push intravenous fluids to keep the mother's blood pressure up as we dissect and remove.

With a very light dose of pain medication, Goldie let us clean and dress her neck wound that afternoon. Sarah spent another hour combing out mud from her coat and trimming her nails as if the show ring were in Goldie's future.

"I'm going to go make some calls." Zoe said. She kept a pink flowered notebook of the names of all potential adoptive families for her golden dogs. She had a handful of foster contacts as well.

"What about that family that fostered those golden wiener dog crosses?" I asked. A randy dachshund had stood on a couch to get to the golden retriever bitch in heat. The resultant litter of ten looked like Twinkies with legs.

"They moved to Japan." Zoe said.

We had a small, round lunch table in our break area. It was just big enough for three people to sit astride and eat, or for one person to read the paper. I came into the room when one of the mature women working in reception had opened discussion with Dr. Max, another doctor at the clinic ironically named Max Maxwell, an enormous man who was a vegetarian because he didn't want to eat dead animals.

"I'll take her home and she can have the pups in my barn," Max said. "Since Jenny's foal died I think she's a bit lonely and distracted in there."

Zoe came in to claim her meal from the microwave and overheard them. "I don't have homes for the pups. I have homes for five if they come out looking like goldens or maybe even yellow labs but not if they're any other kind of cross."

Of course Sarah was in the room as well, waiting to pounce on the now-available microwave to heat her burrito. "Is there a compromise? Can we let her have the pups and we'll keep six? I think my mom would let me foster if there were only six."

I'd met Sarah's mother. There was no way any fostering was going to happen. "Sarah, that IS an excellent idea. The problem is choosing which six survive and whose job is it to euthanize the other five."

"And you're not using my barn as Auschwitz." Dr. Max said. There was simply no response to that. I excused myself.

Goldie stayed overnight. We all expected to see puppies the following morning, but Goldie lay on her side, enormous but relatively content. Mid-morning Vance was in surgery neutering a dog when the receptionist came back.

"Animal control is on the phone. They want to know if we're done with Goldie." If it had been just the neck wound, we'd easily have sent her back to go up or adoption; we'd done it many times in the past with dogs that had mild, treatable wounds.

Above his surgical mask I saw the wrinkles around Vance's eyes tense. The pause in his response was one beat too long. "No, we are not done with her. We'll call when we are." He said firmly.

He finished the neuter procedure. I heard the loud 'snap' of latex surgical gloves coming off. Vance suddenly came back around the corner. "How early do you come in tomorrow?"

"Eight." I said.

"Can you be here at seven?"

"Yes, I can. Are we going to spay her?"

"Yes."

I like to think that Vance asked me to help that day because he knew I could traverse the grayer areas of the job—the ones that don't file easily under 'good' or 'bad'. At one time, while relaying information about a client's needs I remarked in exasperation "People are crazy!" Vance replied, "Well, you are a 'people' too."

I suppose it's just as likely he asked me to help with Goldie's surgery because he knew I was a morning person.

I arrived at 6:30. The rest of the staff wouldn't begin showing up until after eight. Vance helped me put a catheter into Goldie's leg, hook her up to warm fluids, and put a tube in her trachea to deliver oxygen and anesthetic gas. On her back the mass of her abdomen fell against her spine, dwarfing her head and tail. The clippers tripped and snagged on the skin of her belly. Thick, pliant veins ran under the blade as I denuded her, her nipples rough like eraser heads, that I held up each time I had to shave at their base. I didn't want to nick them with my clippers. My hands got moist with milk. I scrubbed the site where her incision would be, scrubbed again, and Vance helped me hoist her onto the table under the surgery lights.

From the Vance's long cut, he pulled Goldie's uterus out of her body cavity very slowly. Each pup, squirrel size in its sack, popped out from its safe nest into the lights, one at a time, like a turgid string of enormous beads. The doctor had his arm into Goldie almost up to his own elbow, blood and tissue sticking to the sleeve of his blue sterile gown. He had to break the uterine ligaments to expose the whole organ on top of Goldie's body, he had to be able to see the arc of both horns of the uterus in order to ligate correctly. Those ligaments, down in the body near the spine, the stomach, and the bladder, make an audible echoing "pop" as they are pulled apart.

Ten minutes into surgery with the doctor working quickly, Goldie was completely filleted. Her load of pups, all twelve, lay outside her body, placed atop the blue drape. "Get the Euthasol." Vance said. He was right. The puppies were too big. Strangling in a dead uterus was inhumane. "Half a mil for each." He said.

Quickly, it was done. I held my catch tub next to the surgery table and the doctor rolled the mass, the heavy thread of Goldie's offspring, off her chest and into my blue plastic catch pail.

I took my cargo, my whole organ with twelve inside to the other surgery table. I spread out Goldie's uterus. In front of me on the table the organ was purpling. I saw one of the puppy mounds shift within the placenta. I pressed the bell against a set of tiny ribs inside the flesh. The little heart was beating. All twelve little hearts were beating. I drew up my Euthasol, pierced through the uterus, between the miniature ribs, getting the bevel of my needle as close to each tiny heart as I could before injecting. I could see through the uterus that these pups were mottled brown, black, and white. They weren't golden retrievers. I listened for their heartbeats again, then turned back to the living.

Dr. Vance closed Goldie's abdomen quickly. Each throw of suture was followed by a short, fast tug, a tiny concession to his distaste for the situation. When he finished he glanced over to where I was tending Goldie, watching her blink and swallow reflexes return.

"Would you like a coffee drink?" He asked me. A drive-through hut was down the road. The morning was steel-grey and rainy. "No thanks," I said.

Goldie revived beautifully. She sat up as I tidied the clinic for the day. Through a window on the far wall Vance looked like a very small figure, his head down, slowly making his way in the rain towards a yellow coffee hut. He held an umbrella covered with the images of enormous kittens playing with balls of yarn.

Within days Zoe had found a loving older couple to adopt Goldie. Though I never met them, I was told the match was ideal.

As is my pattern, I left Dr. Vance's clinic to pursue other interests, but returned seven years later to cover for an employee on maternity leave. I picked up a file for one of the afternoon technician vaccine appointments that named the golden retriever patient as "Sunny". With the vaccine drawn up I went into the room to find an elderly man—perhaps 80—and a golden with a shiny coat, sleek as settled honey. She had a bit of gray around the muzzle and above the eyes. I'd read that she was on arthritis medication. The man put a hand atop the crown of her head as I tented the skin at the back of her neck to inject. That's when I noticed that, hidden beneath her outer coat, she had a ring of bald skin where a collar might be.

"Did you know this was here?" I asked.

"Oh yes, she had an infection before we got her. She was a stray, they say she was pregnant, too. She came into our lives at the perfect time, right after my wife, Margy, was diagnosed with end-stage cancer. Margy had always loved goldens but we hadn't had one in many years so we could travel. She insisted we find a companion for me before she passed. My granddaughter came to live with us that week we brought Sunny home. Her name used to be 'Goldie' but my daughter said 'Sunny' described her better. She really is an angel dog."

Sunny's tail wagged in agreement, her mouth opening as if in a smile. In my mind I could see Dr. Vance ambling away in the rain that morning, bent underneath the umbrella with the kittens.

4

TESTICLES

Men have a special relationship with their dog's testicles. For many guys, neutering is a doomsday topic that, when broached, causes their entire body to seize like a car engine. Long-haired dogs, the ones that hide their modest equipment in wagging shag and furry bloomers, usually have an owner a little more willing to consider the procedure; but the owners of the muscled short-haired dogs—the pit bulls, rottweilers, weimaraners and bulldogs—have a truly terrible time imagining being on the other end of the leash only to see a deflated reminder of surrendered virility. The veterinary field is dominated by women, so the jocularity around the topic of testicles never ceases. Once, while monitoring anesthesia on a spay procedure, I stretched my neck and noticed the ceiling. Adhered to wall above me was a thumbnail size piece of atrophied tissue, a desiccated stalk hanging down like a piece of string. The vet, without looking up from stitching the uterine stump clarified "It's a testicle".

"Bichon Frise?" I asked.

"Lhasa Apso. Karen pitched it up there to illustrate 'balls to the wall'"

Karen was Baptist, sixty-two years old, widowed for eight years, and refused to say the word nipple. But, apparently, her coffee had been strong the day before.

The enmeshed psychology of man and dog is rarely reproduced in male cat owners. Cat testicles don't hang, sway or bounce, they're adhered high and tight, like the small pompom balls children affix to homemade Christmas cards. It could be something about their fuzziness, or the fact that even after neutering most cats appear to carry some baggage in that area, but, whatever it is, cat testes fail to register as great a score on the machismo scale as that of canines.

In reality, dogs don't care of they have testicles or not. They care if you have bacon or a Frisbee.

On the eve of the twenty-first century I was working at a clinic that needed an exorcist. The practice owner had been renowned in the community for his work with patients and his PhD research. The clinic had just moved its business into a brand-new building, specially designed for veterinary practice; client files were still in boxes and the surgery area smelled like a shipping warehouse. Just weeks before my hire, the owner had died from Creutzfeldt-Jakob disease (CJD), an ailment that affects a whopping 200 people worldwide every year (depending on the variant the occurrence can be as high as 1:1,000,000). The remaining veterinarian at the clinic had undergone an organ transplant during veterinary school. She'd maintained her health for almost two decades with extremely low doses of medications that worked with her immune system, but, because of all the stress, she developed a variant of chickenpox: shingles, a terribly painful condition usually spread throughout the body. Dr Illingsworth was lucky in one regard. The outbreak was limited to her right eye.

The clinic manager at the time, and only other licensed technician, was the deceased's wife, Betsy. Buried in paperwork and grief, we rarely saw her.

So, it was into this dysfunction that we welcomed Spike and Ed.

I was pulling large clumps of lint from the dryer's exhaust tubing when Tina came back to talk to me. The problem with Tina was her breasts. They were massive. It was impossible for her to find a set of scrubs that calmed things down enough that male clients could look her in the eye. "Hey, there's a guy up front trying to make an appointment and I can't seem to get a solid explanation of the problem. Can you try?"

Spike McCurry was a man all decked out to be in a Harley gang or on a pirate ship. His face had the start of fine lines at his eyes from wind burn and sun, a funny little goatee at the bottom of his chin, hoop earrings in both ears, and a red bandana covering his hair. We were to later learn that Spike rode up from California with Ed in a sidecar specifically to enroll in the local university's culinary arts program.

"Hi there" I said in my chirpy, client voice. I was sure I saw genuine relief in his face. "What's the story?"

"Oh, well see, my dog, Ed, he has this problem with his . ."

I nodded slowly in encouragement. Clients used every euphemism in the book—or great gaps of silence—to talk about their pet's reproductive organs, around which there was usually great confusion.

Spike went on, "Ed has this . . . swelling . . .".

"You're doing fine, Mr. McCurry. . .".

"One of Ed's balls is swollen." It came out of him in a rush. "The left nut is swollen." Like olives in a bottle, Spike seemed to now be able to spout sentences freely. "It's really hard and swollen, like an orange but his right ball seems fine. If I squeeze that one, it's fine just like . . .".

"Yes! Yes, I think I understand." We agreed that he should come back the following day after he was done with his classes. I asked him to please bring his records from the other clinic in California.

Ed turned out to be a trim, wagging, snorty bulldog not more than a year old. Without tails, bulldogs wag by jiggling their entire back end. Ed was extremely well socialized and well trained. He greeted everyone with drooling exuberance and Spike, with one word, managed to stop Ed mid-stream from peeing on a plastic plant in the reception area. But, indeed, the poor fellow had one testicle that was normal and another the size of bocce ball.

"I forgot my paperwork." Spike looked sheepish, literally hanging his head.

"That's OK," I lied. " We'll get it next time. Can I take him back to the doctor?"

Ed bounced along next to me as we headed to the office. Having the shingles in her eye meant Illingsworth had stunning, radiating headaches. She wore an eye patch. We kept the blinds closed and the lights off as she lay prostrate on the couch for most of her workday. To enter with a veterinary question was like walking into a cave to an oracle.

"The dog with the testicle thingamajig is here."

Ed was crazy with excitement, dancing and snorting around the couch. "Oh heck," Illingsworth said, "Just give me his back legs."

Sitting upright on the couch she grabbed Ed's two back feet and held them up as if prepping the dog for a wheelbarrow race. Too surprised to move, he did, actually, hold still. I watched one of the doctor's hands reach down and gently press the healthy testicle between her thumb and fingers as if looking for a ripe kiwi in the stack at the supermarket. She started to squeeze the swollen one testicle, but Ed bucked out of position.

"If he doesn't want to neuter him, then Clavamox 125, BID, 2 weeks." She said. "And an e-collar if he's fussing down there."

I explained to Spike about the antibiotics and the e-collar, though he swore Ed never bothered the area.

About six days later Spike called. "I think it's getting worse."

They came in, Ed wearing a battered plastic cone, which he pushed into everyone's back legs as a good-natured attempt to sniff us in greeting. Sure as doggy-doo there was no improvement in his unbalanced configuration and yes, it appeared to be a bit bigger and now turning purple. "Is he wearing his cone all the time?"

"Even when we ride the chopper." Spike replied with confidence.

"Dr. Illingsworth is having a pretty good day, let's put you in a room and I'll have her come in."

It was true; the doctor was feeling better than she had in a few weeks. But because of the horrendous swollen bloodshot appearance of the eye she still wore the patch, making for poor depth perception and a propensity to bump into things. Working with her was a bit like working with a frail elder, supporting one elbow and making sure she got into the restroom and exam rooms without incident. "This is the dog with the swollen balls?" She asked as I escorted her to the room.

"Well, it's only one really, he's . . ." then I opened the door to a tense looking Spike and a jovial Ed. Illingsworth hadn't lost her confident handshake and voice. Spike seemed to visibly relax at meeting he plimented her on her eye patch.

"Oh yeah, look at that . . . poor guy . . .". She said, as I supported Ed's rear so he didn't turn around and whack her face with his cone in greeting. "I'd say we should neuter him but I think we should get this swelling down first."

Spike looked at the ground for a moment, then at Ed "Well, doctor, Ed was neutered in California."

It's never good to sound surprised in front of clients, unless they really really want you to. I knew Illingsworth well enough to know the brief quiver in her voice when she was stifling an emotion. "He has been neutered." She stated.

"Yes."

"For Ed's benefit it would be really wonderful to get those records."

"I've been trying to find them, I . . .". Spike began to look and sound like a ninth grader who couldn't find his math homework.

All the while Illingsworth had been squeezing and moving Ed's luggage in circles, which he seemed to be tolerating better than last time. "Do you mind if I do an aspirate to see if there is fluid in there?"

"Fluid?"

"Yeah, it'll make a big difference whether the swelling is filled with blood or serosanguineous fluid. We do it with a tiny needle."

"Uh . . . I have trouble with needles. I'll go—".

"It'll just be a minute, I'll come get you when we're done." I said.

It took Illingsworth a minute to get oriented so that she could actually find her target with her eye trouble. Aspirating Ed's left butt cheek was not part of the plan. She sunk the tiny blue needle into the purpled skin. Ed didn't even flinch.

"What the hell . . ." she said. "There's something in there."

"What?" I asked with some disbelief. Ed was still tolerating things well, only giving off two grunts as if to remind us he was present.

"Have you ever stuck a pen into one of those chunky pink erasers?"

"Not since the fifth grade."

"That's what it feels like." She backed her needle out and actually did manage to aspirate some clear, sticky fluid, the kind of fluid the body produces when it's confused. "Hot pack, have him hot pack this twice a day. And we really need to schedule a biopsy and/or a neuter, depending on whatever the heck happened in California."

Spike made an appointment for "whatever you think is best" the following Tuesday. If we found that Ed needed the whole scrotal sac removed we could do that. If everything looked normal we'd just take a small sample. Spike retained his bashful, scolded demeanor, avoiding eye contact and shifting from one boot to the next.

That Tuesday, with a few snorts and a little drool Ed was under anesthesia with his legs in the air in a truly compromising position. When the doctor cut into the scrotum, however, her bemusement was complete. Out popped a semi-solid, mildly opaque lump. We were speechless, quite literally, for what seemed to be minutes.

"Get a biopsy jar." Illingsworth said bluntly after recovering herself. The lump plunked into the formalin like a tub toy. She regarded the second testicle with pensive annoyance. "Let's leave it for now. It seems healthy." The challenge of having absolutely no idea what was going on made Illingsworth crabby. "He needs to bring those goddam records."

The Fedex guy always stopped by our clinic right around 11a.m. Sometimes we sent out blood to the reference lab, sometimes paperwork to Betsy's attorney, and sometimes pieces of tissue in formalin for histopathology. Ed's little surprise went out the same morning of his surgery. Illingsworth claimed that, even if Spike didn't want a histopath on that lump, she'd pay for it—in the name of scientific curiosity.

Four o'clock in the afternoon at a vet clinic induces the same level of lethargy as at any job. It is the hour of sugar and caffeine, of almost-but-not-quite finished for the day. Betsy was up front when Spike came back to pick up Ed. Only this time he had actually found his paperwork. It was in a blue folder. When Betsy came back, holding the folder out in front of her like an offering, her mouth was open, as if, at any moment, gusts of helium would burst forth and send her spiraling to the floor. She set the information down on the counter in front of us. The very first thing I pulled out was a shiny bumper sticker. It said "I [heart symbol] Neuticles. It's like nothing ever changed!"

"Spike said he was too embarrassed to tell us that Ed got prosthetic implants."

For a few more minutes we poured over the paperwork and Neuticles pamphlet. The testicle implants came in different sizes. You could even order ones with an epididymis so anyone looking extremely closely at your dog's nuts couldn't call the bluff. The founder of the company had a brief write-up about his experience with his own German shepherd, about keeping his dog 'whole'.

"So it's just a tissue reaction." Illingsworth stated with a sigh. "Dammit." I knew her well enough by then to know she was embarrassed to have sent it off, apprehensive about what the pathologist would say. I also knew that scientific curiosity propelled veterinarians just as much as a love of animals; having it blighted by a company that made testicle implants wasn't her idea of a good time.

We did hear from the lab about three days later. They faxed a report that concluded Ed's lump was a hemangiopericytoma, a type of soft tissue sarcoma with a stage II grading. We were to do follow-up, they recommended, in six months to see if it returned and do chemotherapy if so. Illingsworth read the entire thing, broke into a wide smile, and retreated to her darkened cave for a long nap.

The clinic closed just a few months after I was hired there. Betsy fell in love with a new man and moved to the coast to run a fishing charter business with. Illingsworth took a low-stress job at the local army base. The clinic was sold to a naturopath, whose business only survived for a year or two. I drove past that empty clinic almost every day for many years. The realtor sign never seemed to go away.

5

CORNELL

The nurse pulled the needle out of my shoulder. "Come back in two weeks for the second one. We'll do the third one in a month."

"Got it." I said, fingering the piece of tape she'd put over the injection site. I was a new hire at Cornell University veterinary hospital in upstate New York, a geographic area where the rabies virus was endemic in wildlife and not rare in dogs or cats. I'd never forgotten the Zora Neale Hurston's rendition of a human rabies death in her book *Their Eyes Were Watching God.* The illness attacks the brain. It is 100% fatal. No one has recovered to report on how much of their descent into violent madness the victims are aware of. For those who must cease contact and isolate their dying loved ones, however, it is like cutting off one of their own arms or legs. It creates a death before a death from the knowledge of the greatest human punishment: isolation, banishment.

"How much would this vaccination series cost if Cornell wasn't paying for it?"

The nurse paused for a second. "About three hundred, I think. And trust me, it's ten times better than the post-exposure rabies series."

I trusted her.

After the second of the three shots I would run a fever and have flu-like symptoms for a day. Sometimes knowledge is not power and creates only fear. I lay on my back on a mattress on the floor visualizing an army of my immune cells organizing into phalanxes and armadas. *Please,* I was thinking. *Please do your best work.*

Cornell University Hospital for Animals was acronymed CUHA, a syllable that had the deceptive ring of a Pacific island vacation. The building was very tall and square, with top-floor windows that blinked back at the sun like a highrise in the financial district of Manhattan. The first and second floor were the only ones I ever visited, often getting lost in the brickwork maze of the hallways. All the work of the living and dying of animals happened in a very small square footage of that building. The massive volume of world-renowned animal health information that poured out of Cornell had left me with the fantasy that I'd be walking in-and-out of the Disneyland castle every day. CUHA housed its famous Feline Health Center on the top floor of the massive structure. The Feline Health Center did the immunology studies that determined nationwide vaccination recommendations and printed pamphlets that were displayed in clinics from San Francisco to Boston. It coined such terms as "feline high-rise syndrome" and "fur mowing" and it found that 11% of cats prefer to drink water off their paws than put their mouth in the bowl. I was certain that somewhere in the building there was a cat colony and a pile of kittens. The man who founded the feline health center, Dr. Erickson, would often take a break from his paperwork just to ride down on the elevator and say hello to actual cats. "When I started the center I had no idea I'd be stuck behind a desk for twelve days a week," he'd say, a smile breaking over his smooth skin. He emanated kindness and warmth. Even the angry cats would lean into his large hands, sensing their safety. "The best thing about cats is that they understand all the research papers but then they do just want they want. As soon as we think we've figured them out they invent new challenges." I have the enduring image of a

Cornell patient, Mr. Magoo, a middle-aged orange tabby with a white belly and paws. Mr Magoo's pelvis had been shattered when he was hit by a car a fair distance from home. He dragged himself back to his elderly owners and arrived two weeks after they'd seen him last. Maggots had entered his pelvic wound and eaten most of his urethra so that he needed a perineal urethrostomy surgery and some other anatomy alterations. I remember catching Magoo's lively green eyes as he sat in his signature Buddha position during rounds. Even as a chubby cat (he remained an excellent eater), he seemed so small on the grey gurney, surrounded by more than ten veterinary students talking over his care.

Another cat named Tux, a young black and white male, had come to Cornell to have a brain tumor removed that was invading his sinuses. Surgeons had placed a stiff, short, red rubber drain between his eyes that stood straight up like a snorkel. It was my job to to keep his snorkel clear of food and puss, an odious job that he didn't mind.

Dr. Erickson was also an avid motorcyclist. Several weeks after I arrived he was riding on a country road. He swerved to miss hitting a cat. They both died.

It was a hot, glorious July when I started at CUHA. The campus was large, but I could still walk from the hospital to the clinic where I had my rabies vaccine appointment. My new co-workers requested I return from my trip to the nurse with milkshakes from the Dairy Bar. "You can't miss it. It's the kiosk next to the journalism complex with the plastic cow on the roof." It was the 'you can't miss it' that was the kiss of death with my lack of directional sense.

Leaving the health clinic I had no problem finding the Dairy Bar. It, indeed, had a life-size cow figure on the roof, glinting like polished marble in the sun. The treats came from Cornell cows, and specifically what most of us called 'the donut cows' you saw in the pasture as you drove towards campus. They had large rubber rings on their sides. Like puppeteers in a dark theatre, students could reach through the ring and into the cows to get test samples from the ruminants' stomachs.

When I took the ice cream orders from my co-workers, I'd failed to think through how to carry five milkshakes and a double scoop of chocolate ripple back to the ward. I stacked two under my chin, lay two others flat, and simply did the best I could. I began walking. I kept walking. The milkshakes were beginning to sweat; my chin felt moist. Had I walked this far to get to the nurse? Was that tree actually familiar? At some point I came to a parking lot and looked at the wide expanse of my disorientation. I turned around. I walked. I kept walking. By then sweat was wetting the back of my scrubs and the melted milkshakes swayed with each step. I was livid at my stupidity. If someone had offered to help I would've hissed and spat at them. I kept walking. And, yes, finally the seven-story veterinary complex re-appeared like a relative greeting you at the end of a long plane ride. I had to put all the lukewarm shakes and soupy scoops on the ground to fling open the heavy door into the cool freedom of security.

At that time the hourly wage for a technician in my position was dismal. There was a pay differential if I took on a shift from 10 p.m. until 8 a.m. four days a week. I had done swing shifts at other clinics and survived, including emergency shifts that started at 1 a.m. and ended at 7 a.m. It was a needed service; I thought I could do it. Thus began several months of living like a furtive, nocturnal animal. The few of us on this shift were locked inside the monolith of the tall, square building. We were left to function with skeletal tasks, like a beating heart without supporting organs. I was alone on my own ward. My sole job seemed to be administering morphine and antibiotics at prescribed times. At 2 a.m. I walked the dogs that could walk. I cleaned everything I could clean. Sometimes the fourth year veterinary students taking the after hours phone calls would need an opinion about bringing a client in with a purported emergency.

To be alone under fluorescent lights for ten hours out of every twenty-four, to watch the bright wink of linoleum under your feet and become intimately accustomed to the cycling of the ventilation system under the freezers and within the PC computers, all of this colluded to create the sensation that I was hovering above or around my body like a moth. If I could make it through the hours of 3 and 4 a.m., then I would make sure the animals were comfortable and I would walk to one of the windows on a far side of the building to watch the sun hatch through the lifting dark. Seeing that tiny pinch of light was like taking in a deep breath, like being lifted and placed back on a sidewalk next to the rest of the human race.

Anyone who lives long enough can recognize that those early morning hours are the time of birth and death, when life is stripped to the core and at its most poignant. The Tuesday of my first week on that graveyard shift a slim, bright-eyed man in his late sixties came in at 3:30 in the morning. He briefly introduced himself by first name. Then, without further explanation, he went to the unlocked, sliding cabinet under the treatment table and removed a navy blue coverall. He pulled it on, slung his stethoscope back around his neck and breezed out of my ward. The same man showed up on Thursday with a smiling "Hello" and nothing more. He came every Tuesday and Thursday at 3:30 a.m. He never ran out of coveralls. Laundry personnel kept his navy blue worksuit stacked in that one cabinet. One of the day shift technicians that came in to relieve me explained that he was the large animal neurologist, the one with a Ph.D who'd been teaching at Cornell for decades. His lecture classes were during the day, but he met his students for rounds in the large animal wing at 4 a.m. every Tuesday and Thursday because neurology exams at that hour were more authentic. Horses, especially, had dropped their attentive vigilance to stimuli. The autonomic nervous system was left rattling in its cage.

Several years later, when I was back in community practice five thousand miles from Cornell working daytime hours, I shared this same story with a veterinarian who'd graduated from Cornell. "I've forgotten his name . . ." I said.

"Dr. Klausman," she replied. "We loved him enough to meet him there at those God-forsaken hours."

It snuck up on me, the sickness of working those hours. I would get back to my apartment and try to fall asleep around 9 or 10 in the morning, wake midafternoon, try and nap again when most people were sitting down to dinner. Sleep became a monster I tried to manage with barricades and routines, losing more ground every week until I gave up. The Cornell campus had a half-dozen libraries, several of which were open twenty-four hours for student use. On my days off I would roll over at 2 a.m., dress, and drive to where I could see live people engaged in industrious behavior, hear laughter rising over a study cubicle until someone said "hush" and sound was assuaged once more, reduced to the fumble of turning pages and an occasional self-conscious cough.

People talk of "losing themselves" during difficult times in their lives. On one sunny day that fall I decided I needed to do something to animate my psyche, demand a response from my fogged adrenal glands. I went skydiving. It was terribly easy to do for a modest fee and the time it takes to watch a short safety video. A first jump is always a tandem jump. You're strapped to the front of an experienced jumper in charge of pulling the parachute open after the first few thousand feet of freefall. I remember the cows below looked really small. I remember the sudden smack of cool moisture as we fell through a cloud. I remember it all with clinical remove. When checking out afterwards, the pilot asked "Did you enjoy it? I can't tell."

"Yes, Thank you."

The job on the ward did have some interesting moments. It was during one shift in early October that I had reason to be thankful for that rabies vaccine series, not only because it protected me from the disease itself, but because it gave me the sense of security that lead me into the hallway of ghost pictures.

Jill was the last person to leave me that evening. She passed off pertinent information.

"There's a kangaroo in the ward tonight."

I'd almost gotten used to having zoo animals in our care. During my hours of isolation I was in charge of what was known as Intermediate Nursing Care—the animals not expected to die overnight. I was also in charge of doing overnight rounds in the wildlife and exotic ward and sometimes helping in the ICU, which had two staff members staying overnight. "A kangaroo?"

"Her name is Helen." Jill was leading me around a corner of cages. "And she has a joey."

Helen was less than three feet tall; she fit easily into one of our cages. She regarded us with wide-eyed caution. Her feet were like long batons and her arms . . . her little arms moved in front of her like that of a tiny T-rex. The nails on the tips of the three fingers were like that of the crone with the poisoned apple in Snow White. Her right arm had an intravenous line running along the top of it.

"Just make sure her fluids are flowing, and she'll need an antibiotic. That's all you have to do tonight."

"Is she friendly?" I asked. I looked at her liquid brown eyes; she was so far from home.

"I think so." Jill started. "She's also really sick, so it's hard to tell."

I settled into my tasks for the evening, which, that night, included working with some of the inventory. I swiped my employee identification card and hit buttons for some of the most commonly used items. And—this was the magic part—the little cubbies made of glass and metal along the wall would release and extend out towards me, like palms opening. I would count items and confirm their number in the computer.

At midnight it was time for Helen's antibiotic. I approached her cautiously and sat next to her on the bottom of her stainless steel kennel, as if we were about to watch a movie together. She turned towards me slowly. I put the flat of my palm against her pouch; I felt the small joey inside roll 180 degrees. I looked behind Helen, at her massive tail. She sat on it as if it were a third leg, as if she were a tripod. The underside of her tail was hairless and calloused. The top had short, reddish, bristly hair. The tip of her tail rested behind her, curled in a hook shape. She'd been so patient with me so far. I swiveled my body towards the rear of the cage to touch that massive tail, look more closely at how it attached to her body. When my index fingers finally made contact it was jarring. The tail was 100% muscle, like touching a snake or a massive lizard.

Then, from the corner of my eye, I saw a flicker. Swiftly shutting the cage on Helen, I stood. I turned one of the corners in the ward. There it was again, a midair scurrying, a bird, but too low to the ground. I waited what seemed an interminable time before I saw it again and, this time, it landed next to the cotton balls on the counter: a little brown bat, like a kiwifruit with rubber wings, a little pug nose, and tiny gripping hands. How the hell had he gotten through two entry doors, one security station, and down several hallways to enter the wildlife ward?

After considering my options, which included shooting ketamine anesthetic into its hissing mouth, sucking it up into the vacuum system or chasing it into the open door of the freezer, I remembered we had a long-handled dip net with fine mesh for catching angry cats. With my best attempt at stealth, I managed to net both the tiny bat and the canister of cotton balls on the counter, which resulted in a crashing chaos that made the patients sit up and allowed the bat to zip right out the door to the ward.

The overall outlay of the building was something like conjoining squares, Venn diagrams with edges. I knew the hallway that went to the west windows. Net in hand like a flaming torch, I saw another midair flutter and brusquely walked in that direction. I would pause and wait again. There were few hiding spots for a frightened creature in the length of those adjacent hallways. I imagined the terror and disorientation it must be feeling. I saw another dark colored flash and lurched in that direction. I turned a corner.

The hallway I walked into could've been one hundred feet long. Even in the dim light that spilled from behind me and from the adjacent hall up ahead I could make out the parade of dark picture frames on the wall, pictures hung with a level to make them perfect. Not a chair, a table, nor a door to an office was present in the hall. I took a step forward and the motion sensor stimulated the soft, white lights above my head. And there they were. Decades of Cornell veterinary students from the last 110 years stretched from my shoulder to the end of the hall, where a very small white space had been left for upcoming classes. The first photos predated the twentieth century. I paced the length of the hallway in long, gulping strides, letting the faces slide past as if I were on a mechanized walkway at the airport, knowing that many of the people in the pictures had long-since died, that there was no way I'd find out what had brought them to Cornell or what they did after—children they'd had or miscarried, fights with their families, animals they'd saved and guilt they'd never let go of. But that need to know and recognize can be strong. I turned, began at the beginning, and looked into the eyes of each student.

They were young. Even the ones from 1898, the ones that were dead, were trapped in the sepia-forever of resilient freshness. The early photos weren't posed, but of small groups no more than ten, in white coveralls and dark rubber boots in front of a horse or cow. The photos were taken outdoors, where the wind toppled the young men's hair as they grinned in the sun. In 1898 we were a rural country. Most people lived without plumbing. Women could not vote. The knowledge of microbes and medicine was minimal. If people kept companion cats and dogs they were not spayed or vaccinated, they were a sentimental indulgence.

The first woman student showed up in the 1910 photo, also one of the first seated shots not in a barnyard. Half of her smile was lifted up in amusement under a helmet of coiffed, dark hair. They sat her two seats from the center. Her ankles were crossed under a long skirt. There was a gap of a dozen years before the next woman showed up in a photo. The faces of the young men became more posed and gentile, they wore suits and hard-set faces. Even as the photographic quality of the images improved, the candor of the subjects retreated. In one 1930's shot, however, a breathless-looking fellow, still in bib overalls flanked the rear of the group, leaning in. Had he almost missed the appointment with the photographer because he was tending a difficult calving? The longer I looked, the more it seemed that the man next to him held the expression *you smell like cow shit, Frank.*

Women peppered the pictures as the classes grew. There were a few more in the WWII years. The classes became big enough that it was no longer a group picture but a march of alphabetical smiling squares as in a yearbook.

Starting in the mid-seventies, women's faces lept from the grid like kernels of popcorn. The photos were in color, the eye-shadow was blue and the smiles were wide. By the start of the 1980's, the race was on: women were to go from comprising less than 5% of the graduating veterinary classes, to over 70% by the end of the 1980's. By 2005 more than 90% of graduates were women. In one hundred years Cornell had completely reversed its gender demographic, and it was in the company of every other veterinary hospital in the nation.

For a few minutes I had forgotten the bat. I turned slowly in the dim light, expecting to see a flash of activity. I walked toward the windows that looked out into the dark and heard a soft hissing sound. Looking down I saw the bat sitting atop the soil of a large potted plant. The lights behind me turned off. I could see outdoors, into the night, at the rows of sedans and trucks, the horseless carriages of our era. At the turn of the 20th century more than 75% of Americans were employed in farming. In 2005, the percentage hovered around 3%. Farming means cattle and sheep and horses, it means 3 a.m. calls to pull calves or sew horses up, it means rural settings; it means male veterinarians. Compassion had always been a prerequisite to work in the field, but in earlier days the firm knowledge of farm economics had ruled decision making. As we Americans created post-war suburbia, as we put our food production in the hands of fewer and fewer people, as we began to keep small animals solely for recreation, our veterinarians became women. By treating only pets, women also had a better chance of keeping regular office hours and being able to have a family. Women also, in general, more easily accept the lower wage of veterinarians as compared to dentists, human surgeons, and optometrists.

The soft hissing began again; the bat was still there. Carefully, I backed away to retrieve my net from where I'd left it. In the split second it took me to get my net onto the plant he took flight, landing on the wall behind me. I slammed my net against the wall and said aloud "There! Got ya!" I squeezed the net into a little pouch while the creature struggled, and walked towards the door. Throwing open the door, a shrill alarm broke the silence; I rushed into the dark like a criminal with a prize. I lay the net down on the ground, feeling the dew on the grass, seeing its glassiness reflected in the light from behind me, and hearing the bone-shaking call of the alarm. I began untangling the bat as fast as I could, the alarm still peeling out. It was at the very last moment, as I removed the last tangle of net webbing from around one of his wings, that he did it. I felt his little teeth curling into my index finger, an inoculating sting running up my arm. Reflexively I raised my hand into the dark and shook, shook again until he detached. He rose into the dark, clear night because he belonged there, and an arc of my own blood rose against the sky in his wake.

I did, on subsequent nights, go back and visit the students in the pictures. I was drawn to the oldest photos, the animated faces that invited me in. Each time I noticed something more. I made up stories about them. I exquisitely studied that first woman in 1910. She was my friend, alone in the mob, teetering between economics and nurturing, the meridian where statistics meet case history.

I left Cornell ten months after I started there. It felt like everything died. Helen and her joey died, cats with brain tumors died, dogs used for stem cell research died, zoo tortoises and miniature horses caught in grain threshers died. Despite the endoscopy, MRI, bone scans, waterbeds, oxygen chambers and more, we could not save them. There were no puppies and kittens and wellness exams. There was no narrative to the animal's visit. I never met the owners or took the x-rays or blood work. That was done in a different section of the hospital, more like human medicine, the Henry Ford specialization of skills. Each animal was reduced to a clipboard with circles around what time I should inject or withdraw fluid. I had been reduced to someone I no longer recognized or liked.

"About 10% of people find they just aren't cut out for working in a teaching hospital." My supervisor said kindly in my exit interview. Who had done that research? What was their sample size and age of participants? Still, that is the best place to leave it: "aren't cut out". During my time at Cornell I felt cut out. I visited that data plot on the graph that says isolation creates depression and reduction of life into the shallow, diseased machinery of eating and shitting and sleeping. There is no vaccine to protect a person from that knowledge of needing others. There are only choices and consent.

interlude: "Don't be such a vet tech!"

If you make it through this whole book you will not find a single dog or cat bite injury story. I am fairly astute at reading the body language of animals, but I am also a wimp. There is always someone braver to call upon when an animal is growling or cowering. Countless poetic analogies could be made from the fact that my veterinary injuries have all been self-inflicted and primarily limited to my right eye.

"The first cut is the deepest" and happened in my twenties. It was midafternoon and I was so tired that day it felt like I was wading through concrete. Hard-copy radiographs were still the norm and filing them required holding the film up to the light to find names, numbers, and dates. I reached into a manilla-colored x-ray sleeve and whisked out an 11x17 film. It hit my eye. How? Something about the weight of the film and the laws of physical motion account for its arch up into my eyeball. I thought I was an idiot, I rinsed my eye in the eyewash station and finished the day.

On the other side of midnight I woke up feeling like a hot sword had impaled my right eye. I stumbled to the phone and called a trusted friend, who had me at the emergency room in a flash. The memory of relief after they instilled the numbing agent has given me great compassion for patients with eye injuries. "Wow." the doctor started (never good). "You shaved off a nice chunk of your cornea." Bedrest, eye drops, a pirate eye patch and my discovery of audio books ensued. I got a laugh out of coworkers when I wore safety goggles to work on my return.

Five years later, while working at Cornell, I was asked to take a golden retriever to the hydrotherapy room and give him an enema; his seizure medication had made him constipated as well as non-ambulatory. He lay there flaccid on the grate, his business-end toward the faucet while I proceeded. In a flash, he started again with a grand mal seizure. The irrigation instrument, now covered with fecal residue, went right into my eye. It didn't hurt, it was the middle of the night, and I was the only one in charge of my ward, so leaving work to find a human doctor wasn't on my mind. When I awoke the next afternoon the entire sclera of my right eye was cherry red. The lid was mildly swollen, but the primary problem was that I looked terrifying. A zombie apocalypse had entered through my right eye and was incubating there. I had some antibiotic eye drops and ointment I started before work.

My supervisor saw me that night "My God! Have you seen a doctor? Tell me you aren't being a vet tech about this!" She was referencing the proclivity for technicians, as low wage earners often with poor health insurance, to muck about medicating ourselves. Technicians, and veterinarians for that matter, will treat vaginal yeast infections with canine ear medication, use topical lidocaine to do their own sutures, and give themselves intravenous fluids after a hard night of partying. I once had a sweet older veterinarian hand me his nineteen-year-old daughter and asked me to take a radiograph of her foot to make sure her toe wasn't broken.

I had one other eye episode for which I have no explanation. I worked with a clever, funny, and charming young mother who was also embroiled in an abusive dating relationship. She had taken a particularly bad beating that involved a punch to the eye. While grumbling and speculation roiled from other coworkers, she was good-natured and frank about it, not attempting make-up cover-up or evasive lies about the cause. It was the next morning I woke up and, without incident, the same scleral hemorrhage I'd experienced at Cornell had returned. I ran into my coworker at the store. Her own injury was turning a grey-blue as it healed. "I don't know..." I said when she asked about my startling countenance. "I think it's sympathy eye."

6

SYMMETRY

"**D**avid gave Mary a kitten!" Alexis blurted, after appearing in the doorway of my boarding school dormitory room. I was engrossed in finishing an essay for the African history class I'd elected to take as a senior. It was a non-traditional high school. "It's orange and white! It's tiny!" Her mahogany-colored eyes, always exuberant and expressive, were extra-wide with a tinge of alarm. As quickly as she appeared, she angled her body and signalled me to follow her into the hall.

Alexis was fifteen-years-old and she barely cleared four-feet in height. Her hands and feet, however, were normal size for her age. Her thick fingers and deeply creased palms, coupled with the way she gestured in grand, winging arcs, created the sense that her hands were catcher's mitts. At times she delivered such frank and incisive commentary you expected to hear the *whump* sound of a baseball slamming into its perfect home. "When people look at me funny and wonder if I'm a dwarf, I just tell them I have Turner's Syndrome, which means only one X instead of XX or XY, so I'm really special and really short." She had encyclopedic knowledge of her anomaly, which helped her pre-empt people's observations and help them feel more comfortable. "Have you ever heard that if you tie an Italian person's hands behind their back back they can't talk? Well I'm Italian, *and*

I have this thing related to Turner's where my elbows rotate a little outwards. My nana says I can almost fly when I get excited!"

Alexis' single X chromosome came with other burdens. One evening, when her roommate Mary was in the shower, I went to ask her if she needed extended time before lights out to finish her math homework. She was reaching for her shirt. The pale, narrow ribcage startled me. Her nearly translucent flat stretch of skin where breasts should've been reminded me of young boys at the swimming pool, electric with energy but frail and knock-kneed. Frozen where I stood, I started to apologize for walking in, but she knowingly relieved me of my burden by saying "I got my math done on time tonight!" She wore her broad smile and reached for an elastic to wrap around her hair. "I think I can be ready for calculus by next fall. Do you want me to to do *your* hair tonight?"

The feel of Alexis French braiding my hair in the evenings, before the dormitory hall got quiet, was so mesmerizing I couldn't make a sentence while she thinned, clustered, and wove her pattern. I had trouble believing there was any pleasure left for her in the act, as if a finite amount of satisfaction were allotted to the task and I had taken it all. Her own hair was chestnut brown, long and very thick. There was a straight stiffness to it, however, something about Turners and the keratin formation, she once explained. It was not hair most girls wanted.

While there was gregarious magic to Alexis' personality, it was also patently obvious her parents had nurtured her, against the odds, into a confident person. She unabashedly loved her family, not the most common thing for the boarding school set. Her father and mother, though separated, came to visit often. "My favorite thing to do in the whole world is go to the beach with my dad." She'd articulate the word "beach" with a cozy affection that left you longing for your own sense of blanketed safeness. At seventeen, acutely aware of the the need for belonging and the hard-levied rules of beauty, I felt both jealousy and revulsion.

"Where did David get a kitten?!" I easily left my desk and my essays to follow her. I was the hall monitor for ten freshman girls. Add a kitten and who knew what would happen.

Freshman didn't get to choose their roommates; random pairings were considered one of the character building assets of boarding school. Alexis had been matched with Mary. Classically beautiful, Mary had long golden hair with a wave that didn't kink up or frizz or require styling products. She had petal-pink lips, and a gentle slope to her hips that matched her perfect set of B-cup starter breasts. But Mary acted as if she'd been dumped into the shell of her body by sudden accident. She made no eye contact unless distinctly encouraged. I had to lower my own head, find her, and attempt to lead upward with my gaze of assurance. Her hands were always tugging the front of her T-shirt away from her body to disrupt detection of her silhouette. She hugged herself with her arms over her chest and the heels of her pink sneakers would press together like closed scissors. Her paranoia about gossip went so far as reluctance to leave her room during social events or take phone calls on our one hall phone (beyond brief, whispered dialogue with a parent). She made it clear that even having someone else utter her name was anathema, almost the way some religions decree that we should not call out God by name.

I followed Alexis into the hall.

The school put the freshman girls on the top floor of a nineteenth century building without elevators, assuming all those stairs would function to admonish young teenagers to remember books and school supplies. It also put us under the dormers, so that our lounge area had low, irregular ceilings. Mary was huddled in the smallest corner with the dimmest light. She clutched a cheerful pink Candie's shoebox without a lid. A ripped piece of green towel hung over the side, its frayed edges brushing against Mary's acid-wash jeans. She recognized the sound of our footsteps on the old floorboards. She trusted us, so that when she did look up, her face was stark with emotion. It was the face of someone drowning, someone who'd just come to the flash of reality that they were going under—fear, surprise, an attempt to gather up all other thoughts, memories, spoken and unspoken words. Her cheeks were flushed. As we came closer, her eyes melted into tears without blinking.

No sound came from the shoebox. Alexis and I sat beside her on the tattered couch like bookends. Inside the box was a kitten with a little triangle, alien face. She had long fur in patches of orange and white, but even the fluff couldn't hide her emaciation and dehydration. Her three-inch tail was matted down with mustard-yellow diarrhea. She tipped her head up in a palsied way to see the looming shadow of my face and let out a strangled, weak, squeaking noise.

"Mary," I said quietly, not taking the liberty of putting my arm around her but gesturing with my hand I was willing to do so, "where did you get this kitten?"

Her voice didn't break, but two tears rolled into the box as if they'd been dropped through the roof of the building. Her gaze stayed locked on the kitten. "The boys had her in Lathrop dorm. They've had her for a while." She paused, reaching to stroke the kitten with a light, whispered touch. "David had her. . ." her mouth trembled slightly. She recovered "Brian had her before that, and he got her from Damian who brought her from his cousin's . . ."

Mary had allowed Alexis to wrap her short arm around her. I'd watched the two of them bond during their time together. Despite their great physical differences, and even their differences in demeanor and confidence, they shared an emotional sensitivity. On weekends they'd take the school's van to the mall together, or I could find them downstairs in the TV lounge watching one of the Disney movies on VHS Alexis had brought from home. They'd be laughing with each other, Mary speaking in her most audible voice. I even caught Mary whirling her arms about, taking up space with hand gestures the way Alexis did so easily.

Only once had I seen them come close to a fight. Mary had borrowed some nail polish and Alexis had begun to put on the same color. Mary was incensed at the idea they would match. Their voices escalated. Alexis was the one to concede, choosing instead to wear a cornflower blue nail enamel for the next week, which drew further attention to her hands.

Quietly I asked Mary "Has this kitten seen a veterinarian?"

Mary hadn't yet looked at me. She lifted a corner of the towel and attempted to clean some of the stool off the kitten's tail. I let her have her silence for a little longer. One second. Two seconds. Another wet tear fell into the box. The tear was large enough, and the kittens so frail, it was a relief that it didn't land in the creature's fur.

I began again "Mary, has this...?"

Without rising, and without giving any warning, Mary broke. She began yelling.

"EMILY HAD THIS KITTEN! Emily had this kitten FOR AN ENTIRE DAY two days ago and then she GAVE HER BACK TO DAVID!!" She thrust the box into Alexis' lap and stood up, pacing along the small area in front of us "Emily SHOULD HAVE HELPED her!!!" Mary's eyes came to rest on Alexis, who sat as stunned and silent as I was. Emily was also a young woman on our hall, also a freshman.

Mary spoke again, more quietly, her eyes moving between my frozen helplessness and Alexis. "The kitten was on this hall needing help and Emily. Did. Nothing."

"Wait . . ." Alexis said, trying to clarify. "He gave it to Emily first? Does he want to date Emily?!"

I'd been vaguely aware Mary had a crush on David. Emily was a distinctly different animal than any other freshman girl. She was taller than I was, perhaps 5'6" or more. She had stone-heavy breasts we'd all seen many times. A small, blue heart-shaped tattoo rode low on her belly. Those first few weeks of school, when the warm evenings were filled with crickets and the open windows brought in the night sounds of patrolling security guards in golf-carts, Emily would shower before bed. Then she would move her desk chair to the window, take a seat and plant both her feet on the ledge, completely naked.

I witnessed this behavior once, one evening when walking down the hall when I noticed Emily's naked shoulders above the back of the plastic chair. I saw the tops of her thighs running to the apex of her knees, and then her bare feet, toes wiggling and stretching apart from each other, gripping the sill. Her roommate, a sweet, unassuming redhead named Beth came to me the next week and said it had been going on every night since the start of school. "Can you tell her to stop?" Beth's face was in pain as she spoke. "And she tells me stuff, stuff I don't want to know about being on the pill, and her uncle raping her and a bunch of other things."

I spoke to Emily, mumbling something about trying not to make her roommate uncomfortable. She seemed bored with me. I was the one straining to communicate with all my seventeen-year-old skills. Emily finally responded with distaste "It'd be nice to have a roommate who *wasn't* a virgin… but it doesn't matter much anyway, I won't be here long."

That had been several weeks ago. She's stopped her evening window nudity, but the weather had also changed. Beth had reported Emily shaved her pubic hair bald after that.

Mary stopped her pacing abruptly. "David would date her." She said, moving back to her place on the couch. "He and Emily had sex."

"Nooo…" Alexis exhaled.

"Yessss." Mary parodied.

On Alexis' lap the kitten made another strangled cry and struggled to right itself. Mary produced a small bag of dry kibble and a jar of chicken baby food, which she tried to ease into the side of the kitten's mouth with a broken popsicle stick, but most of it caught in the kitten's fur. The baby food was the same color as the stool on the kitten's tail. Both substances shared a fruity, fetid, rich, warm odor that would, much later in my life, come to signal the death of infants.

At the time it seemed impossible to tell any campus adult that we had an animal on the hall. Had we chosen to take the risk, an adult would've immediately thrown us in their car and taken the kitten for emergency care despite it being so late in the day. We found a phone book and a veterinarian we could walk to the next morning while everyone else was eating breakfast. None of us aptly described the kitten, beyond that it "was sick". The veterinarian on the phone told Mary to keep it warm, keep trying to feed it, don't give it milk, come first thing in the morning. We agreed Mary could keep the kitten in their room, under her bed, the little secret binding the three of us together.

Evening study hall in our dorm ran after dinner from 7-9 p.m. on weeknights. Lights out was at 10 p.m. Once in a while one of the adults in the dorm apartments would notice lights still on at eleven and would walk onto the floor and speak sternly. We were good girls, if only in that we responded to adult requests promptly and without friction.

The school was in eastern Pennsylvania, several hundred miles from where I grew up in Connecticut, but in a verdant, agrarian setting that I'd read about in books and seen in pictures. I wanted a school with a barn, with horses and the smell of hay. A few other places in Vermont and Maine had equestrian centers, with massive indoor riding arenas and young women in shiny, leather riding boots and britches that looked painted on around their perfect figures. The school I chose in Pennsylvania was run by Quakers, the Religious Society of Friends, long known for their liberality and eschewing formal ritual for direct meaning. People went down the barn in jeans and T-shirts, borrowing riding shoes from the office with windows as opaque as baking parchment because they hadn't been cleaned. Quakers discussed things. If a student was caught with an illicit substance they were driven to a twelve-step meeting and had multiple conversations with campus adults. If they were caught having sex they'd be taken to Planned Parenthood to review birth control options. Talking, there was always lots of talking.

The hall quieted at the time of lights-out. The three main perks of being in charge of a dormitory hall were that I could have a mini fridge, a TV, and I wasn't beholden to lights-out. For the second time that day, Alexis arrived in my doorway. Her long, blue nightgown flowed over the narrow perimeter of her body, brushing her ankles. Bright eyes, large hands, thick hair and a perplexed, apprehensive look on her face were what I remember. She sat on the very edge of my bed.

"What's sex like?" She asked. "Is it as great as they say?"

However the messages had reached me in the late eighties and early nineties in the high-powered East Coast culture, the message was this: sex is power, sex is maturity, sex is self. To remain sexually inexperienced into your college years was wimpy and naive. By seventeen I'd had sex a few times, but it wasn't until I was in my twenties that "as great as they say" showed up.

"You don't have to tell me . . ." Alexis blurted a few seconds later.

"No . . .". I simply hadn't expected that question, nor ever been asked to encapsulate an experience. "It's nice to be that close to someone, to have them know who you are, to be able to express things."

"With your body." Alexis finished.

"Yes".

"What's love like?" She asked. "I mean, how do you know?"

I laughed, then she did as well. We could both reference titles from songs that begged the same question. Like the question about sex, my answer—at that age—was, by necessity, premature. "For me it feels like wanting to wrap someone up and always keep them safe."

She considered this for a while, then "But you can feel that for anyone, even without sex."

"Yes." My voice trailed off as I considered the implications I had not before.

"Well, I have to make this decision, see..." and her hands reached up into the air between us to help explain ". . . so . . . I can put off puberty and see if I can get taller, or I can take the hormones to get breasts and hair, but I have to stay this height. Mom and dad say it's my decision, but I wish it weren't. I don't want to be four-feet-tall my whole life, but I don't want to look like a boy when I'm a senior. I get crushes, too, and Mary is, like, the only one who believes me! Then I start to think a boy likes me back and I get my hopes up, but then someone asks him and it's not real. So I don't know if it would be different if I just started the hormones. What would you do?"

To this day I do not have an answer to that question. I listened to Alexis for a while, doing as much affirmation as I could, trying to help her clarify her thoughts. The Quakers call it "active listening". The process resonates in your head long after the conversation ends creating more of an "active learning" sensation.

I had the kitten dream for the first time that night. I was in charge of raising a tiny, grey kitten who was terribly hungry. He went to a shallow dish of moist food, and I watched his miniature pink tongue flick back-and-forth over the mound of nutrition. Despite his exertions, none of the food made it into his hungry mouth. In the dream, I then realized it was because it was only the kitten's head at the dish. The rest of the body, attached to the bottom jaw, was missing. I left the head at the dish and frantically searched my house. Piled in my closet, amidst leather shoes, was the remainder of the warm, living body. With great excitement I went back to the head at the dish and tried to put the two pieces together, angling and jamming and turning and attempting different techniques. The dream always ends before the two pieces go together.

Our little white and orange kitten was dead by the morning. We wrapped the cold, stiff, emaciated body in the towel. The three of us skipped breakfast to hide our emotions. Mary and Alexis, wept large, greedy tears on the floor of my room while I tried to be a stoic adult. I called the veterinarian and told him our kitten was dead and we wouldn't be coming in. We talked briefly. He was kind. I remember him saying "This happens a lot; it's not your fault. People think these little guys are ready to be out in the world at four or five weeks. Some kid—no offense—usually grabs the kitten from the rest of the litter and tries to play mom. They get passed around, like what you described. Then they're too far gone."

Mary, Alexis and myself marched out to the edge of the campus later that afternoon, Mary cradling the tiny body of the kitten. With three soup spoons borrowed from the cafeteria we dug a shallow hole in wooded area Alexis chose. From the Quaker tradition, we replaced prayer with borrowed silence.

Mary wanted to confront Emily, but Emily finally got her wish and left school unannounced. No one saw her pack a bag or leave. One weekday she was getting ready with all of us in the morning, and in the evening she was gone with all her belongings. Beth was greatly relieved, of course. Several months later she would get a new roommate, a statuesque Texan with long black hair and an exceptionally loud speaking voice. She was a vociferous advocate for virginity and she introduced us all to Little Debbie Star Crunch snacks. By the end of that school year Mary was dating David. We were told he was a good kisser. Almost no one on the hall ever mentioned Emily again, pointedly avoiding the topic in a way that cemented her indelible presence

Alexis waited. "I want to be five-feet tall. The doctor said that's still possible. I need to learn patience." She said. I was still learning that the people who can say such things already have more of that virtue than the rest of us.

Later that year I purchased my first pre-owned computer for $50. It was an old Macintosh, with a black screen that I filled with a blitz of green letters. I started my first novel, naming the succession of floppy disks after Winnie the Pooh characters. I filled my cube fridge with green apples and peanut butter, which made up 80% of my diet for several weeks. In April of that year I walked over to the library and began the printing process on the begrudging dot matrix printer. It's prolonged stuttering, unzipping sound brought the librarian over. "Whose class is this for?"

"Well ... it's not really for a class...".

"Oh." She stopped. "You're writing a *book*." She seemed frightened for me.

Everyone at school made a big showing of resenting that our school mascot was a tree. These were Quakers, after all. The sports teams suffered the most, in their brown and buff school colors with the arboreal symbol lacing out into branches at the top and roots at the bottom. But after all this time, looking back at my final high school years at that school is like circling the trunk of that tree. I was already deeply planted as a veterinary technician, a teacher, and a writer, but I didn't know what fit where. For years after I took things and tried to jam them together. I would have the dream about the kitten head repeatedly in the next decades, any time my best efforts didn't yield the results I wanted. Now, I can go back and examine the fissures and scars in the woody skin of that old tree. I can scan down its length to see how it is grounded. I can see a disruption of soil to the left where a thick root surged up, a divot on the right side where a small rodent went burrowing. I am able to see sex and death and the reality that things forced into the light before their perfect time can not survive. There are too many answers that are not ours to know and, like the tree, we can't run away.

7

PARASITOLOGY

When I was in technician school I had a parasitology teacher who loved to exclaim, "It may be poop to you, but it's *my* bread and butter!" Mr. Finn was a tall, wiry man in his early sixties and had the added intrigue of being unabashedly homosexual (in this regard it was helpful that 98% of his students were young women). Some days he'd come to class in large floppy sunhats with poppies along the brim. He used his arms like wands, occasionally giving a balletic leap when describing *Taenia taeniaeformis* bursting forth from its egg packets. He was excellent with anecdotes and metaphors. "What is an obligate parasite, you ask?" He swept his arm over our heads in a god-like inclusive gesture. "You are, my dears! While you are in school you are obligated to get your financial nourishment from an outside source. Often your parents." He was also the master of the dramatic pause and wink. We went through an entire eight weeks of parasitology classes without the man ever saying the word "anus". The word's conspicuous absence loomed larger every day until one bolder classmate wanted to agitate for truth. Finn had just finished explaining that clear adhesive tape—not the more common matte finish tape—would not only pick up any pinworm eggs present on the horse, but also allow us to immediately affix the sample to a microscope slide. My classmate's hand shot into the air. "Sir, where exactly *are* we putting the scotch tape to pull up and test for pinworm eggs?"

"Well, my dear, if you don't know by now I—".

"I *don't* really know, exactly . . .".

He looked her square in the face and replied. "The hoochie."

It's possible to get a four-year degree solely in parasitology and still only skim the surface of nature's creativity. For the complexity of the lifecycles in most of these ugly dependents it is a wonder that they survive at all, much less flourish. A true parasitologist would take issue with the term "ugly", preferring something like "resourceful" or "adapted". (In the 1990s one company did try to upgrade parasites to "cute" by creating wide-eyed cartoon characters like Tickles the tapeworm, Digger the head louse, and Holly the blond-haired hostess. I had the Tickles pencil case and Holly lunchbox). Some parasites need as many as seven intermediate hosts, those other species they infest as a stepping stone to get to their next growth stage. In most textbooks a colorful wheel represents their life cycles. Mosquitoes, rabbits, turtles, muddy river bottoms, birds of prey, snails and others ring the periphery as the hapless hosts to unannounced guests. Snails always seemed to be the biggest losers; it was so common for them to be a host that we began to think of them as burger joints along the highway. Fortunately, because technician school is about applied science, we only had to memorize the life cycle of the forty-five parasites most likely to be seen in our future jobs. This included the map of a maturing protozoan infection of gorillas, just in case we took a zoo position.

Not every parasite is found in the digestive tract. Some are parasites of the lungs or liver or nasal passages. Most parasites of clinical significance in companion animal veterinary medicine are, indeed, found in poop. And, while the vast majority of parasites cannot infect both humans and pets (they are "species-specific"— a human tapeworm can't infect a dog and vice versa) a few key species can be shared between humans and animals. Along with the complexity of their life cycles, the creatures are inspired to act differently within different species. For example, if someone steps barefoot on dog feces infested with hookworm eggs, the eggs hatch at the surface of the skin and the tiny larvae begin their migration to the human eye. A few larvae always lose their way and get stuck in the liver, kidneys or lungs. This is called visceral larva migrans. Such things are treatable. The subsequent nightmares are not.

Beyond the issue of public health there are a great many reasons to look into feces: dog shows, boarding kennels, camping trips, in-home daycare, diarrhea and owner peace-of-mind. In a single calendar year a veterinary technician may run over a thousand fecal tests. Multiply this by the $25.00 dollar charge and . . . Mr. Finn was right, poop is the bread-and-butter of the veterinary field.

For the most common fecal test you only need a pea-sized amount of stool from the pet. Invariably owners send in the whole yule log for good measure. Receptionists come back holding the bag or Tupperware several feet away from their bodies so we can immediately tell they aren't bringing baked goods from a client. If it's a particularly noxious sample even longtime receptionists forget where the laboratory sink is—where they need to leave their gift for us—and we point them in the right direction while they make fanning motions in front of their face. To the bottom of a tiny plastic cup we add the feces, then a liquid zinc solution that makes all the parasite eggs float up to the surface like helium balloons. We put a slide cover slip over the top like a mortarboard. Then we wait 20 minutes, put the coverslip on a regular slide and prepare to be dazzled. Mr. Finn used to wax poetic that under the microscope we were looking for the distinct "glow of life" to differentiate a parasite egg from plant pollen or an air bubble. We would find it in the ropey corona of *Toxocara canis*, the bundle of golf balls inside the ova of *Ancylostoma caninum*. Most often there was nothing on the slide at all. As students we were so primed to see *something* that random scratches on the microscope lens has us calling to our peers for a second opinion. We would take hours or decades to review one slide before giving up. While fecal analysis can be a great moneymaker in private practice, it can also be intensely boring.

The average veterinary technician stays in the field for five years. By then the bloom is off the rose; they've seen it all and have physical injuries to show for it. Those that stay longer develop a protective crust, either covering heartbreak with humor and sarcasm or refusing to overextend themselves in any way, running from the building at exactly 5:01 p.m. regardless of circumstances. Whenever they have the chance they delegate to fresh technicians, the eager-to-please curious young women who have few boundaries around what they were willing to do. At one point, that was me: eager, interested, the ultimate "yes-gir.". In that era of my life, when paired up with Dr. Doran on her shift, the woman who treated all clients as family members, we were an infamous anything-goes duo. Do your giant millipedes have lice? Bring them in. Do you want to be present for your iguana's tail amputation? Sure. Does your duck have a fishhook in his mouth and your eight-year-old veterinary wannabe needs to help? Great. Would you like to say the Rosary over your guinea pig in private? No problem. The oddities and eccentricities were our specialty.

And so it was that on a particularly bleak February afternoon a small woman in a red parka walked into the clinic. She had light brown hair cut in layers to give it lift and frame her small face, her pursed lips. She had something of a Slavic accent, a thickening of consonants and clipped nouns. I was told that when she came in she was agitated. She didn't have an appointment but was deeply concerned and pled to be allowed to wait for an opening.

Doran was affixing a label to a bottle of arthritis medication when Susan arrived in the back and started "Triple D is on line three." (This was code for 'Dr. Doran's dad'. They were close; he called often.) "And there's a woman up front—not a regular client—who really wants to be seen as a walk-in."

"What's her issue?"

"Don't know, she won't say, but she's got something inside her coat." Everything from kittens to ferrets to turtles came to the clinic inside coats. Surprisingly, terrorism never occurred to us.

Doran's finger poised over the blinking phone line. "OK. Put her in a room." "Dad?"

Once, Doran did actually pick up the wrong phone line, looking for her father in the owners of a maltese with bad skin.

I was in charge of laboratory samples that day. We all helped each other with whatever tasks were needed, but it worked best to have only one person running and recording samples, dealing with shipping labels to outside laboratories and reading cytologies. The lab was a little alcove sheltered from the main working area, like a small office where you could be queen for a day. It was your moment to master your own workflow and, as a senior technician put it, tell veterinarians they could calm-the-fuck-down and wait until you completed more critical tasks before getting their results. It was hard for any of us not to feel proprietary when running lab.

After only a few minutes in an exam room with the mystery woman, Doran came back to the treatment area. She came right towards me. "So . . . this woman is just afraid that her dog has worms."

A mild, tingling sensation began in the middle of my spine; I braced myself for the request.

"And she wants to be present for the fecal."

The request seemed awkward and unusual but not as bizarre as the guinea pig and the rosary. "Uh, OK." I made sure my hair was in its barrette and that there was no blood on my scrubs. I waited.

A minute later Doran came back. The woman still had her parka on, holding the conspicuous lump beneath. "This is Maya" Dr. Doran said to me.

Maya's one free hand was cool and dry when I shook it. She nodded but said nothing.

"I'll let you two at it." Doran turned and walked away.

Maya seemed reticent and disoriented. I started. "OK, to run the tests we need to get some samples."

As if pulling a precious archeological urn from behind a curtain, Maya brought forth an industrial-size pickle jar from inside her coat. It held at least two gallons. The content was clearly a mixture of feces and water. Beyond simply being foul, it wasn't the right kind of sample.

"This is it?" I asked stupidly, as if she had the real dog shit in her pocket and this was only a bluff. I don't recall what she said in answer, I remember only that her words were foggy, a little distorted, and with that thick accent.

For the test it was important to get a very small—but very dense—fecal sample on the end of an applicator stick. Diluted feces had a high rate of false negative readings; we'd miss picking up parasites if the animal was infested. But remembering one of the veterinary adages "if you can't give them what they need, give them what they want" and I unscrewed the lid on the pickle jar. Reflexively, I drew back.

Technicians, without their own consent, become experts in distinguishing the odor of dog and cat feces from that of all other species. At one clinic I worked at the male office manager would go into the lab to fart, thinking that with the other fecal samples no one would be able to tell. He was quickly identified, reprimanded by one of the technicians (his *wife*) and given his own sequestered office space. I can still hear her saying "We can *tell*, Don!"

Over time we are also able to smell infection and bacterial overgrowth in feces, urine and ear cytologies. This can be handy, but is rarely a transferable skill set if we choose to leave the field.

"What has your dog been eating?" I asked the woman. With my nose wrinkled so intensely, my voice took on a weird, metallic sound, even as I was trying to hide my disgust. The odor was rotten, too sweet, acrid.

Again, I can't recall the details of her muffled response. "I'm going to have to dump this in the sink to get my sample." I informed her.

Fortunately, there was a hood over the sink with a fan I could turn on. I poured the contents of the jar into the sink very, very slowly. 'Bacterial shower' is the too-descriptive term for sending rods and cocci into the air with agitated movement. The feces was almost completely composed of long, stringy material—not worms—but definitely like pulp from citrus fruit.

"Has your dog been eating a lot of fruit?"

"Fruit?!" I *do* remember that particular, articulated response from her.

"Yes, grapefruit . . . maybe oranges?" I gave her some time for a response, but none came. "I don't think I can run the test of this sample."

She'd found a tongue depressor and was pushing the material around in the sink in a way that reminded me of scientists doing delicate work in the rock at a dinosaur excavation site.

"My dog??"

"Yes" I was reaching for my own tongue depressor, hoping I could find one dense piece sufficient for my test.

"No, mine." She said without looking up.

There was a delay in my thinking. My body reacted first; my skin became hot, my head felt light, nausea swirled into my gut as I looked at the wide scatter of brown pulp in my lab sink. A technician's relationship to animal waste is parental. We don't spend more time with it then we must, but different forms and abnormalities elicit compassion and worry. We don't enjoy it, but we're willing to put on a glove to sort through poop to see if the animal passed the offending toy, rag or household item. We clean up tails, tushes and feet while hoping for cleaner days to come. *Human* waste is only one thing. It is shit.

"This is yours?" I asked.

Still not looking up, still trying to unearth the Pleistocene with her tongue depressor: "Yes." She replied.

I backed slowly away from Maya, still trying to organize my thoughts. Doran was at the computer. I flew to her and shouted in a hushed tone. "Did you know that stool is HERS?"

Doran's eyes darted up to mine, visibly reflecting the same thought-delay I'd grappled with. "What?!"

For the next twenty minutes there was a hushed, but animated interchange between Doran, Maya, and the admitting receptionist receptionist. Maya's voice rose with an argumentative panic. Doran threatened to get the police involved before Maya agreed to be escorted out of the building. The receptionist lightly touched her elbow to inquire if she had transportation and a place to go. Maya shook her off, her elbow rising like an offended wing as she turned away in frustration.

All of this still left me with the messy, egregious violation of my technician's oath in the lab sink. I put on two pairs of gloves and a surgery mask to scoop the stuff into the trash. I used so much bleach no one was allowed into the lab for an hour. Upon finishing my task, I stepped from the lab and blurted without thinking "I feel like a fecal whore!"

Had I the inkling that anyone was looking for a nickname for me I would've been more judicious with my outcry. As it happened, for three more years, my moniker at that clinic became Fecal Whore which, thankfully, was eventually abbreviated to FW.

Maya made the papers the following day. She'd gone into a middle school science classroom and helped herself to a microscope with which to examine her stool. Fortunately, her notoriety did get her some appropriate psychiatric care.

For all my resented intrusion of human waste into the inviolate realm of veterinary medicine, a few years later there was some solid payback.

As in many licensed professions, technicians are required to do a certain amount of continuing education annually. Sometimes it was useful to travel to large conferences where renowned cardiologists left you yearning for an MRI as you gazed at the cream congealing atop your cold coffee and wrote things in the margins of the published proceedings. There was always better take-home loot at the bigger gatherings. One veterinarian I knew got held up by the drug-sniffing dogs in the airport because of all the sample bacon-flavored medications in her suitcase. But other years it was nice to skip the annual frenzy of travel and earn continuing education credits closer to home.

One year I helped with the details of bringing a prominent parasitologist up from Purdue Veterinary School. A friend had a friend who knew a friend who had him as a teacher. He arrived at our airport with a small cooler of different feces with known infestations; it had been his one carry-on item and he'd had to sign a waiver with airport security that he wouldn't open it mid-flight.

Finding a cost-effective venue to host the event had been a challenge. Ironically, it was the classiest hotel in town that was the best bargain. They wanted to put us in the Gold Room. I had been to several wedding receptions in that room, drunk champagne and eaten filet mignon. I explained to the event coordinator what we were doing. All she heard was 'veterinary' which sounds really fun and cute to many people. The room was nice and large, with plenty of room for maneuvering around microscopes for a look-see.

On the day of our event we had more than a dozen microscopes out, as well as a long buffet of feces for sampling and viewing. The professor had started with a lecture, and we'd been indulging in a wet lab for over an hour. A side table with a white tablecloth still had coffee and a few danishes on a sticky silver tray. We'd long-since failed to notice the odor of our doings. After a period of time in the field many of us end up with blunted olfactory senses anyway. Sure as shit, in the middle of the event, a young couple and the event coordinator came to see the room as a prospective wedding reception site. There was a quick pause in the rambling words of the couple's tour guide as she finally understood what we were doing in their celebrated Gold Room. But, like a stage actress used to quick recoveries she pursued her speech and began talking even faster. Her words moved from a brusque trot into a canter and then a gallop. The prospective couple, wide-eyed and silent, were backing slowly away. I went to talk to the event coordinator afterwards, to thank her for the perfect setting. Her eyes were wide during our entire conversation and she wouldn't come within four feet of me. Later, as I told this to one of the technicians at the event who knew me well, my friend said "What? You didn't shake her hand and welcome her to the secret FW sisterhood?"

8

AMPLITUDE

"**G**et the diazepam, dammit!" Dr. Prue was hunched over the seizuring black Labrador on the floor of the treatment area. The couple that owned the dog were standing behind the four of us, watching our tense-mouthed scurry with wet faces. The dog had already been in the middle of a grand mal seizure when they came flying through the front door, trying to hold on to his writhing body wrapped in an army blanket. The receptionist had bypassed the exam room, pushing open the swinging door to treatment, bellowing the "Seizuring! Incoming!" Julie was trying to get an intravenous catheter into the front leg but it was like trying to thread a needle while it was in a blender.

"You want a butterfly?" I asked her quietly. I was referring to a type of catheter that more easily hit the mark difficult situations. During emergencies my voice instinctively takes on the tone of golf narration, as if I'm trying to bring peace and control back into the room.

Julie's gaze slid off to my direction, so I know she'd heard me, but she was still fully engaged with what was in her hand "FUCK!" She threw the catheter off to the side while blood streamed down the dog's legs from her attempts

"Rectally, give it rectally, dammit!" Prue yelled angrily.

The owners are right here, I thought to myself. *Get it together, Prue.* Dr. Prue was tall, thin and gray-haired, with wrinkles around his mouth and on his forehead. I'd been doing some temporary work for his practice for several weeks by then. Prue loved business management, the oversight of the clinic as an economic machine, not the mushy chaos of people or even the science of medicine. When not under stress he'd developed a facsimile of competence with human relations by virtue of being in the veterinary field for over three decades.

"How much valium?" Eric, another technician, asked with some trepidation

"'Till the seizure stops!" Prue's intonation contained the accusation of *you idiot,* even if he hadn't stated it.

I watched Eric, with palsied hands, navigate a syringe around an emerging turd and shoot what seemed like a drinking glass full of valium into the dog's rectum. Within minutes the mucosa had absorbed the drug and the frothing, paddling, vocalizing dog slumped into silence. Julie immediately went back to working on getting a catheter into one of the legs now that he was still.

Emergency veterinary work is one of the fastest ways to kill your adrenal system and skew your sleeping hours. It's one of the only jobs where you can get a call at 1:30 in the morning that says you're late to work. Work comes in lulls and rushes, with high emotions and impressive traumas: cats caught in fan belts, dogs that had been running and impaled themselves with a tree limb, dogs that ate bread dough now rising inside them, owners who backed over their pets. When you turn your shift over to the next crew you never say "Have a good day," you wave goodbye while wishing them "Easy and fixable!"

"Ruger" was the name of the dog we stabilized that night. Dr. Prue took the owners in a room to get some history while we worked at lowering Ruger's body temperature (elevated from so much muscle activity), drawing his blood, and finding a kennel in the observation area.

Prue came back. "He's only four," he said, looking at the dog, not at us. As I mentioned, Prue had just enough people skills to get him in-and-out of an exam room with clients so that they didn't think he was an ogre, but with his staff he didn't feel obligated to even try."Didn't get into anything . . . Give me the bloodwork when it's out." He retreated to his office, where no one was allowed to disturb him.

Nothing was off with Ruger's blood except his glucose level: 36. That's low, almost low enough to cause seizures. "Feed him." Prue commanded, unalarmed.

Ruger ate like a champ. Labradors are infamous for their appetites. Most of the time they don't stop eating until they are just minutes from death; we've managed to genetically engineer them so they have no satiety center in their brain. Julie did get that catheter in and we began intravenous fluids. Ruger was sitting up and watching us go about routine work with other patients. Almost imperceptibly he swayed, like a sailor too long at sea.

Nearly three hours after we admitted him there was another slamming sound as Ruger's skull hit the side of his kennel and he went into another grand mal seizure. With access to a vein we could stop it quickly with valium. Prue calculated out an oral phenobarbital dose and one for potassium bromide to begin the work of actually preventing seizures. "Idiopathic epilepsy" Prue mumbled. This type of diagnosis is often called 'idiot-pathic epilepsy' because it states in Latin that we have no idea what is causing the condition. "They can contact the hospital about doing an MRI if they want." Prue said this dismissively, beginning to turn away from us and back into his cave.

At that time, in that area of the country, access to an MRI machine required contacting the human hospital for a guest pass. When owners really wanted or need answers for the seizure activity and if they could pay the large fee, it could be done. I'd once crawled into the back of a veterinarian's SUV with a German shepherd attached to an entire anesthesia machine to ride over to the human hospital. The dog had intractable seizures and we didn't want him having one en route. Unfortunately, the few MRI scans I've seen done in pets still don't clarify a diagnosis.

Two hours later Ruger seized again. We gave a higher dose of valium.

Ninety minutes later, more seizure activity.

"Julie . . ." I looked at her as she drew away from Ruger's I.V. line with an empty syringe of valium. "What about an insulinoma?" In emergency work there can often be excessive downtime. There's always a list of chores and cleaning to do, but at some point you are left to crack open veterinary trade magazines, which include interesting case histories. If Ruger had an insulin-producing tumor no amount of food was going to keep his blood sugar high enough to prevent seizures.

Julie knew what an insulinoma was, and she knew how we'd confirm it."Test his blood sugar again? You go ask him . . ." Clearly she wasn't up for marching into Prue's office to suggest a diagnosis. She shook her head "He'll figure it out eventually, anyway."

One hour before the end of my shift I had to feed the dog in the kennel above Ruger. I had to microwave the food so it would be extra smelly and enticing. Ruger clawed at the cage bars get to the food, his eyes locked on the prize, panning upwards until the bowl was out of site.

Within a half-hour Ruger seized again.

"Fucking Christ." Prue muttered when I stood in the door of his office to tell him.

Tentatively I asked "Can we test his blood sugar again? Could he have an insulinoma?"

"The dog ate, right?"

"Yes"

"I wouldn't worry about it." He said.

As I matured as a veterinary technician I became better at leaving my concerns behind me when I left for the day. Our veterinarians always have it worse than technicians, with all their take-home research and late-night treatment revelations. But as in all health fields, there is a lot of birth and death and you simply can't care deeply every time. As you get older the cases that do break through that compassion blockade carry some extra weight. Ruger's case showed up right before my two consecutive days off, and I was certain

Prue would come to his senses in how to treat the dog. But Ruger had, indeed, died. The owners had asked for an necropsy and Prue had sent some samples to the lab. When I arrived that day, Julie told me with an eye-rolling fatalism, "It was an insulinoma".

After the news, I needed a few extra minutes to myself before I clocked in for my shift. I went up front to the bright, windowed world of reception to sit next to a ficus plant and open Cat Fancy magazine to the kitten-of-the-month. Our receptionist was stumbling through a conversation with two women up front who spoke Tagalog as a primary language. One was clearly the mother, an older, small woman doing all the talking. The taller girl quietly held a small white dog in her arms. Our receptionist was studying a little folder and went on "On this vaccine record I don't see the last rabies. Did your dog have rabies?" The older woman's eyes widened and she gestured to her daughter "No babies! She not married!" Things were explained and even I laughed along. Other entertaining client vaccine misunderstandings have included a sincere belief that the dog doesn't need the distemper vaccine because "there's nothing wrong with his temper!" My personal favorite, however, came from a young veterinary assistant who always called the bordatella (kennel cough) vaccine "that bordello shot" invoking tightly-drawn red velvet curtains and illicit encounters in black-laced secrecy. Vaccines remind us of all the things we can do for pets, instead of all the things we can't.

Not long after Ruger's death, a beagle came in with a laceration on its hind leg from running into a wire fence while playing with bigger dogs. The owner, a woman in her thirties who worked as a nurse in human medicine, wanted to be present for Beanie's anesthesia and suturing. Once we were ready, with Beanie comfortably asleep and cleaned up, I went to get a sterile pack of instruments and a little stand on which to open them for Dr. Prue. He came in with his gloves on, while I was carefully pulling back the corners of the outer cloth wrap on the instruments, revealing an untouched and sterile inner wrap that Prue would open. "See?" Prue said, turning to Beanie's owner, "it's so easy even a vet tech can do it."

He was not joking. There was no safety net of a warm rapport to create irony, no relationship in which to place such a comment. The nurse glanced at me with mild concern, while Prue acted like nothing had come out of his mouth at all. Then, I did something I have never done before or since. I abandoned an anesthetized patient. Calmly, I turned around, signed out of my shift four hours earlier than scheduled, and went home.

It wasn't without some strenuous internal conversations that I returned the next day for a regular shift as if nothing had happened. My palms were sweaty even as I walked tall and cool. I heard Prue's distinct footsteps coming out of his office. Then he called me over. I did everything I could to stay calm. Prue was standing in front of another Labrador, not unlike Ruger in color and build, but this dog had the yellow-orange jaundice in his eyes that was the hallmark of a struggling liver. Dr. Prue did not look up at me as he narrated. "This dog hasn't gotten into anything. He's got a bit of a fever. He walks like he's arthritic but he's eighteen months old." There was inquiry in Prue's voice. There was a long silence while I tried to gauge what was happening.

"How long has he been this way?" I finally asked.

"Since his owner came back from hunting."

In that area of the country an enormous percentage of men go out to "moose camp" during the first week of September. It had been a very rainy season this year. At Cornell, under such circumstances, they tested any dog with liver issues for one particular illness.

"Have you tested for Leptospirosis?" I asked.

Prue glanced at me. There was a touch of apprehension in his as his gaze met mine. Then he said "That's a very good idea."

The beauty of Leptospirosis is that it is treatable. It is very treatable.

Another time I had to stake my claim to competence was in a milder situation with a younger doctor. Dr. Sizsle was in his late twenties and built like a brick, both mentally and physically. He was in constant search of new ways to bend the world to his will, but in an adolescent, lurching way. His sentences were always brusque and short. For these reasons his favorite area of veterinary medicine was orthopedics. He would grudgingly do soft tissue surgeries but they were, well, *soft*. In an orthopedic surgery he had license to crack bones and use a drill, to use a sterilized hacksaw and wire twisters then zipper up an incision with a cascade of staples. He once went through three staple guns. Click. Click. Click. Click. All I could think about was having the dog come back for the technicians to hold him down and remove those damn things . Even the diagnosis and treatment of internal medicine cases was something Sizsle avoided. "Too non-specific" he said once. When short on veterinarians Siszle was forced to take wellness exams and puppy and kitten exams. He'd bring a squeeze-ball on those days and march, head down, from room-to-room.

One day, one of his rooms contained a very ill four-month-old kitten. The kitten was anemic. He had eye discharge and a slight fever. There's a thumb-size plastic test kit, a little like a human pregnancy test, with which we test cats for the feline leukemia virus. Two dots, yes. One dot, no. It's always the first thing to test for in a young, sick cat.

The ten-minute timer in the lab went off. I looked. Two dots.

Sizsle came over with the kitten's chart open in his hands. "I missed it earlier, we can't charge them for this test because the kitten was just vaccinated."

"What?" I asked.

"He was vaccinated ten days ago. False positive."

"Leukemia doesn't work like that. Vaccination doesn't affect the test." I stated.

"Yes, it does."

"No, it actually doesn't."

A formative experience in my veterinary journey had come several years ago when my beloved three-year-old cat stopped playing. She was profoundly anemic. Her liver was twice the normal size. We did a blood transfusion and many different treatments. We could only manage to get a diagnosis of feline leukemia by taking a bone-marrow biopsy from her frail little hip, and she died one-month later.

Like many people who've lost loved ones, in order to resurrect my sense of control, I became an expert on feline leukemia. I published a five-page paper in Veterinary Technician Magazine through which technicians could earn education credits by taking the test at the end. It didn't bring my small friend back, or reveal more than how the disease was cunning and powerful, but it did qualify me to contradict Siszle.

"The kitten has leukemia. If it shows up on this test that means it's circulating in the peripheral blood and looking for places to land." I told Siszle, as his face began to color with frustration.

Diagnosing feline leukemia always left me crestfallen. Like people with HIV, some cats can live long lives and never show signs. Once they are sick, however, the outcome is rarely good. I was spending a few moments petting a post-spay puppy when Siszle returned.

"You were right," he said tersely. "And Andrea told me about your paper. Congrats on that."

I'd been as frustrated with Siszle as he was with me. He had minimal skills in communicating sensitive news to clients or helping them understand yet, even when I offered to speak to the owners of the kitten, he dismissed the idea.

An intrepid young veterinarian had dated Siszle a few months prior. The romantic energy at the time was distracting for all of us. They'd done an admirable job breaking it off while avoiding work drama, but Dr. Brown was not above a few quietly articulated cutting jabs at Sizle's personality when she could get them in. "Would you ever guess . . ." she started, ". . . that man is afraid of hamsters?" She had my full attention. She looked directly at me. "Even pictures of them."

By 5:30 we'd done it. Siszle's entire front and rear windshields were papered with pictures of furry, buck-toothed rodents harvested from veterinary magazines, trifold hand-outs and empty bags and bottles. For good measure we put a little grass hay and a rodent water bottle in the driver's side door handle. Siszle made no sound when he finally walked to the parking lot. Peeking out the back door we saw him stop abruptly mid-stride. He then gently removed the water bottle, but got into the car without removing a single one of the pictures. The car engine turned on. Then, with the force of a cannon, he backed and sped off, sending hamster images snowing into the rush of air behind him.

"It seems like . . ." my friend's voice came over the phone several years later, anchored in our self-reflective conversation about personal boundaries, "there's always one last big drama before we make that leap in our growth . . . not to put up . . . with . . . bullshit, y'know?"

The years and experiences had stacked up to bring me back to the city where I'd initially done my technician training. I was moving into the teaching field, but had jumped in to do some relief work at a local clinic while waiting for the school to start.

I was thrilled about being able to help fill in at a low-cost hospital that made affordable spaying and neutering a priority; they even did international work in areas of the world that needed it most. The man behind the machine of the organization, Dr. F, had won awards and published papers. He was easy to find over the Internet.

For lack of space, I sat on a sturdy stack of canned dog food for my "interview" with the lead technician, who sat on an overturned bucket a few inches away. "We do a lot of surgery. Are you good with that?" There was a flat, apathetic demeanor to her that was eerie, as if she'd just gotten news that a beloved family member died or that she hadn't slept in more than 72 hours. It was unclear what my hourly wage was, but doing some work there seemed like a good way to use my time during a summer of transition.

It was another week before I had a start date. I had to call them about four times to get the date set. The lead tech was either unavailable or, when someone checked with her, she didn't know yet. I would come to understand that dealing with Dr. F was like working with a wild animal. You'd have to choose your time for interaction based on subtle nonverbal cues, times of day, knowledge of behavior patterns and anticipation of his stressors. It was roulette.

Once inside the clinic in my scrubs, I discovered the locus of the chaos were the five surgery tables clustered in a small room with fluorescent lighting. Due to the thrift and speed of the surgical action, everyone wore gloves for procedures but didn't bother with masks or gowns or more traditional forms of sterility. There were no surgical lights. Gauze sponges, paper waste, organs and pieces of tissue littered the floor. "Don't fucking clean! They do that at night!" Another technician yelled, catching me bending down on my first day. I jerked my hand up from the floor. "Here, throw a towel over it" She tossed me a surgical towel to place over pooling blood as she hoisted a patient off the table in front of her. The blood was from a whiplash-fast splenectomy and I had almost slipped in the smear.

Another technician bullhorned from around the corner "Who's the asswipe that didn't label cage 36?! Fucking cunts can't get it straight...". She then mumbled something else before flying into the surgery room with a young Labrador in arms, a dog almost as big as she was. "Who are YOU?" She asked, glaring at me, still holding the dog on the table and reaching for a syringe. I told her. "Yeah, well I'm the grumpy bitch." I instinctively put a hand on the puppy while she moved the anesthetic machine closer.

A receptionist came in brusquely holding some papers. "There's a Mexican prick up front who's pissed we never called him back about his dog's broken leg...".

"Five-hundred dollars" Dr. F hollered from the far surgery table, where he was taking out his second spleen of the morning. He was well over six-feet tall. His muscled legs stuck out of running shorts and finished with rubber sandals. His sun-leathered skin was burnished with mandala tattoos and viney plant images. He had shaggy gray hair.

The receptionist continued, resentfully "He doesn't want the dog neutered when you fix the leg."

"Then tell him he's an asshole and no deal." Dr. F said. "Jesus H Christ! This damn thing… ". Dr. F hauled a football-sized tumor attached to a spleen out of the dog and into the light. "Somebody get over here!" He was trying to angle the trash can with his foot while avoiding the blood-soaked towel I'd put down earlier.

The receptionist ploughed onward. "I told him that."

Dr. F bellowed back "Fucking tell him again…" An assistant had run under the surgery table and was frantically trying to help while Dr.F yelled "Shit! No! Don't move the fucking trash can, move the towel….Tell him again the dog needs to be neutered or he can pay out the ass at another clinic." The receptionist turned and left.

Our Labrador dog had already been induced and I was ratcheting open his jaw so The Grumpy Bitch could place an endotracheal tube. On the surgery table behind me I heard the snarl, then the deafening metallic scream of a cat.

A different receptionist with a large carrier shot through the door "They brought us fifteen this time. Fucking fifteen, can you believe it?!" An assistant took the carrier from her. A quick peek from over my shoulder while I tied the dog into position for his surgery told me the carrier was full of kittens.

"Sexed?" Dr F asked, still elbow deep in a dog and ligating vessels. Male kittens are easy to castrate. Female kittens need a spay.

"No."

"Then stop being a lazy cunt and do that."

She left, presumably to the kennel room.

Dr. F ran the show, but another half-dozen international veterinarians helped. Bulgaria, Japan, East Africa, Germany, California and other countries were all represented. A dazzling number of surgeries were performed every day. Never in my life have I ever physically worked as hard as I did there. Never in my life have I experienced both the volume and frequency of the words cunt, fuck, fucker, fucking, asswipe, asspimple, prick, shit, Christ, snatch, pussy, dick and a myriad of old-school racial epithets. Such words were emotionally tangled together by everyone, as if forming a collaborative pidgin

English delivered with sick affection. Most of the support staff at that clinic had been there for many years. *Something* was tying them together.

I was there when they were undergoing building renovation. There was an afternoon when we continued with the gory frenzy without electricity. Dr. F lived upstairs. At one point his apartment's bathroom was the only one available. Opening the door you were immediately confronted with the odor of alcohol. One wall had special shelving that hosted a colorful assortment of international liquors, their sparking vessels rising towards the ceiling like a temple.

Due to construction, we also ended up stashing the highly infectious parvo dogs upstairs. We were often too busy to get up to them before the hemorrhagic diarrhea started leaking out of the kennels and down the stairwell. Despite every effort to contain it, we took the virus with us, and it spread to other patients.

On Saturdays we did very cheap vaccines. The primarily Spanish-speaking clients would begin lining up outside the building with their pets early in the day as if waiting for a rock concert. "Each visit should take no more than ten minutes. Don't talk to them, just stick the pet. If they ask you a question, tell them you don't know, they should come back and make an appointment." Making that adjustment in my behavior was almost impossible.

Three weeks after I started I was handed a handwritten check that was half of what I'd been imagining. It would've been alright with me if any of the other things I cherished about working in the veterinary world had been present: expressive compassion, curiosity, kindness, patience, and most of all, laughter. Tears, there were plenty of tears. There was bosom-heaving sobbing in the xray room or outside the back door where everyone went to smoke, but there was no laughter. Entering that building every day was like walking into the belly of a volcano with rage-roiling guts. There were several small fights between employees every day, grumblings and half-shouts about things not done or done wrong or done too slowly. They were truncated arguments; shut off before the work of resolution could cool the issue.

A film crew showed up from a television station to make some great reality TV. Dr. F was famous enough. Most people reacted to his animal-oriented persona the way I had before my first day: *what a wonderful dedication to helping animals and people!* But with great height, comes great depth. Amplitude: the magnitude of difference between the variable's extreme values.

The veterinarian from East Africa was the man everyone had decided was a problem. They'd decided he had poor patient care, didn't make follow-up calls and was lazy. The evidence was slippery, and it was primarily rooted in differing cultural interpretations, but no one had time for that kind of analysis. Dr. Bwanye was putting pins in the comminuted femoral fracture of an eighty-pound dog. I was holding the toes of the affected leg in the air while standing on a bucket (there were lots of buckets in that clinic) so he could get a better angle. Dr. F had been doing office work and management tasks most of the morning, which meant the camera crews were in his face, not ours in surgery, until he came storming in.

"Bwanye, I just got off my third fucking phone call with the live-in bitch married to the owner of that fucking Pit Bull you did last week—the ACL? He died, *you fucker*, that dog died!"

"I deed te surgery as specified… I calt heem for ta post-op…" Bwanye had remarkable composure when the lids blew off the pots. He kept his hand on the drill he was using.

From another surgery table a technician yelled "He's lying! He never called! That dog's dick owner kept calling about needing antibiotics for his dog, 'cause that new cunt up front didn't send them home with him, and every time I talked to him he said he never heard from…".

"I med te calls end I felt te medcation…"

I switched arms. Holding a limb in the air for an extended time creates a burning sensation in your bicep. Most clinics have a hook from the ceiling or a mounted surgery light you can hang it from.

"YOU'RE A FUCKING LIAR YOU PIECE OF SHIT!" The technician screamed at the top of her lungs.

The cameras were rolling. They angled in behind Dr. F. Dr. Bwanye kept working. When he used the drill, sloppy bone and tissue debris spattered both our faces.

"She's not too far off, you fucker! We need to get this bullshit resolved and I'm tired of…." He threw the folder he was holding on the floor and began screaming a level of invective and insult I had never heard before except in cinematic renditions of the criminally insane. The technician behind him helped. The cameras kept rolling.

Is this really happening? What is this? Who are these people? I can't recreate what was said, even a fictional approximation. I stayed where I was, holding the leg of that dog. A burning heat infused my scalp and the roots of my hair had an unpleasant prickle. My face became hot, moisture springing under my lower lids. I took long, deep, slow breaths. I had the acute urge to urinate, and squeezed my legs together.

It ended. Everything must, eventually. Dr. F left, taking the cameras with him. Two other technicians went out the back door to smoke. Dr. Bwanye and I finished the surgery.

After extubating Bwanye's dog and leaving him recovering on a towel, I went to visit the kittens in the small kennels in the hallway. The females all had tiny red star stickers between their ears so we could tell which gender we were grabbing. Some still bobbed their heads, listing and tumbling along the cage floor as they recovered from anesthesia. I was squatting by the bottom cage, folded up and in on myself like a tight rock. I don't think Dr. F ever saw me as he came down the corridor alone. He took long, loping strides down the corridor. His muscled body was heavily hunched, faintly echoing the illustrations of bewildered human ancestors—Cro-Magnon man or late australopithecines. He was muttering, mumbling to himself. All that I could make out as I felt the breeze from his body moving past me was "this fucking shithole—".

It occurred to me that it was the shithole *he* created, the building he was paying to renovate, the two dozen employees, the bills, payroll, TV show, interviews, international obligations. He had created the trap he now found himself in. He couldn't stop. If he stopped, it all did. The dream was real and good. The execution had become its own execution, the highs and lows flatlining.

At the end of the day I went to the lead technician and said I could finish out the month, but not longer. Her violent words from earlier were still fresh in my mind. I was prepared for outrage.

Instead, in slow motion, she nodded solemnly "This is not an easy place to work. You should, if you can, get out."

9

BRINGING PIZZA TO THE CIRCUS

Many smaller communities lack a veterinary emergency service dedicated to providing care when other clinics are closed. Hospitals are left managing overnight crises on their own. Similar to the way the well-meaning era of American Prohibition actually introduced more bad elements into society than it prevented, such towns have cultivated bizarre superstitions about who takes the pager home and is on call: You want to be the technician on-call on a Monday night because no one ever needs you because they all needed you on Sunday. If you are on call on a Saturday you should have your adult beverage before 8 p.m. so you can be sober enough to do whatever surgery is coming your way at midnight, but if it's a Saturday after a holiday you're probably safe from getting called in, so imbibe with impunity. Major emergency surgeries like cesarian sections and GDVs always run in threes, so check with the previous night's on-call tech to make sure you aren't in the middle of a streak. No one wants to be on call on the Fourth of July, Thanksgiving, Mother's' Day or Memorial Day weekend, during moose hunting season in September when dogs get shot (something about beer, firearms, and triggering up in the low-light of dawn and dusk), and never, ever accept the pager on the night of a full moon.

Up until the 1990's Dr. Vance's clinic would house a senior veterinary student for several months at a time and leave them in charge of taking calls. It's unclear if this saved anyone any hassle, as the primary thing veterinary students are missing is confidence in their decisions, but it certainly screened out random diarrhea questions or those who thought their cat was dying of a painful cancer but actually turned out to be in heat. The cure for that condition is a spay. I took a call like that once. The client was relieved, but asked "So what can we do before the spay appointment to shut up all her yowling in the middle of the night?" I'd learned a response from one of the most creative and unique veterinarians I'd ever met, and I reiterated Dr. Aimes' advice "Throw her in a cold shower. She'll spend the rest of the night grooming herself."

Dr. Aimes was the veterinarian who started a stand-alone after hours veterinary hospital in the small northern town that I know well. She enjoyed belly dancing, science fiction movies, herpetology, yoga, herbal medicine, and bringing home-baked treats to every veterinary clinic within a 100-mile radius of the city center in a famous annual Halloween reverse-trick-or-treating ritual. (If I read this aloud to her she'd finish it with ". . . and long walks on the beach!") We'd use our pre-dawn hours on October 31st to spread out all the cookies and candy on the surgery table and make sure all the goodie bags had the same contents. Other clinics opened when her service was closing, so delivering the treats during business hours gave us a chance to see inside the other hospitals, query people about the outcome of some of the cases we'd transferred, or share cautionary tales about certain clients. Aimes was always in costume and there was always lots of fake blood. She was the daughter of a small-town human doctor, who, as I remember her describing, always rigged up their family vehicle with big speakers from which to to blare the 1962 song Monster Mash as they drove to different trick-or-treat destinations.

She ran the emergency clinic out of an old house. At start-up she'd purchased a 400-pound radiograph machine "from the Civil War era" which was named Matilda in an effort to cultivate fondness for the behemoth. Because the house was constructed with the fortitude of a Cracker Jack box, though Matilda was on wheels, it was imperative her enormous bulk sit on top of a steel beam that extended through the basement and into the foundation. The basement had a damp, wormy odor and housed a washer and dryer, medical inventory, mounds of decorations for every holiday real or invented, a paper mache dragon head, and eclectic gifts from clients and employees. Velour blankets with elaborate pictures of wildlife, purchased at the local fair, hung on the walls to prevent visualization of the lousy foundation. While switching the laundry or taking inventory you could hear every footfall above you, in any direction, by the sigh and creak of the floor boards.

The electrical system in that building reminded me of the time I spent in sub-Saharan East Africa. Working outlets could easily be overloaded and were hidden in odd places, requiring extension cords that tripped both the circuits and our feet. Flashlights and backup generators were stashed in odd places with the resourcefulness of an alcoholic trying to make sure she never ran out. When Aimes finally got an electrician to open up the walls and bring things to code, they found that the walls were insulated with trash—old mattresses and torn jeans, newspapers and other highly flammable substances.

Running a clinic that is open from 6 p.m. to 8 a.m. on weekends and 24 hours on weekends and holidays means you are at work for about 100 hours a week. Aimes would try and sleep every night in a small bunk over the office computer, but had perfected the art of hearing the phone ring and being able to articulate doses for aspirin, diphenhydramine, famotidine and simethicone without rolling over. Everyone with an animal emergency is apprehensive about the cost of treatment, and everyone wants to get out of their companion animal worries by spending as little money as possible. At the time I worked for her, if you did the accounting math, it turned out that Aimes payed herself something like $3.00 an hour. The wages she paid her support staff would only be considered "fair" by regular practice standards, but they were a generous stretch in the financial health of her practice. But then there were the perks, like being asked which Star Wars movie I wanted to watch with her in the middle of the night, eating the ham, turkey and trimmings she brought in on holidays, and the midnight metaphysical discussions of spirituality and dating, which often left me feeling like I should pay her for a therapy session.

Before my time working for Aimes I was pathologically shy about answering phone calls from clients. By the time I moved on I could deflect, diffuse, and decode nearly any client question or mood. There was the man who called and spoke in monotone that his dog had just been hit by a car and was certainly dead. But he was a good dog. Was there any way he could "collect his seed" post mortem to breed another dog like him? There was the hysterical woman who called because her rottweiler had just eaten the cat's newborn kittens. As tenderly as I could, I told her there was nothing I could do, but if her dog developed gastrointestinal problems from such a rich meal she should consider coming in. There was an equally hysterical woman whose dog ate her *own* puppies. Dogs, cats and mini horses also managed to ingest marijuana, heroine, glue, coffee beans and light bulbs. Another woman called because there was a moose with a broken leg in her yard. That's an issue for Fish & Game. *No, I can't promise they won't shoot him.* I distinctly recall staying on the phone for more than an hour on a Sunday afternoon with one woman who needed to talk about what her gay neighbor was throwing into her yard to poison her dog. I tried every leave-taking phrase and tonal shift in my voice to try and end the call, to no avail. Ultimately, she ended up discussing her estrangement from her gay son, and, weeping, made a donation to our Angel Fund with her VISA card. Emotionally drained and almost limp, as soon as I hung up I saw Aimes behind me. She said, smiling, "You should really charge an hourly rate for that kind of help."

When Aimes was forced from R.E.M sleep or deeply fatigued from a long weekend her communication filter with clients went out like a street light. She'd use terms far above their heads or phrases we'd coined during treatment that qualified as inside jokes. She'd use personal anecdotes about yeast and bladder infections, Brazilian bikini waxes, and finding whole corn kernels in your stool.

There wasn't anything wrong with her words themselves, it was the mismatch of what she chose to say in front of which client. A bewildered seventeen-year-old trying to get her mother on the phone may not recognize the phrase "pharmacologically enhanced". An elderly woman whose cat's eye infection has just been diagnosed as herpes and chlamydia may not need to hear "Don't worry, your cat hasn't been having sex in her eyeball, it's a different herpes than we get." Aimes had a standard cause-and-effect anecdote she pulled out when referencing the mysteries of working with non-speaking patients. She'd seen a female basset hound named Missy more than four times for acute bladder infections. The dog had been on special food, had its urine repeatedly cultured looking for pathogens, and had been on three different antibiotics. The infection would always clear and return in a few weeks. The same client had a little male, intact poodle dog. Someone accidentally stepped on the poodle during a holiday gathering and the dog came in holding his right front paw high in the air. Aimes immediately noticed a foul odor from the dog's mouth and found what is so common to all toy dogs—end-stage dental disease. Only brown-black calculus kept the teeth adhered to his brick-red, inflamed gums. "Oh," the owner replied, surprised yet dismissive. "I suppose his mouth is so bad because he keeps licking Missy's vulva when she has her infections." Aimes suspected she had her answer. The poodle was giving the basset her bladder infections with his oral explorations. It wasn't confirmed until the little guy went, had all his teeth pulled and his gums rinsed with disinfectant. He still licked Missy's vulva, but Missy never had another bladder infection.

Because the building was initially a house it wasn't designed for privacy. All the rooms were the size of modest bedrooms and the doors had the density of Styrofoam, providing just as much sound barrier. Emergencies tend to catch people off-guard, so a single pet was often accompanied by several people—the five children one of the sisters is watching, the family on a picnic, the couple who live in the area escorting out-of-town visitors with their yorkie. Romances had been both forged and finalized in that front room. Acquaintances who'd lost touch over the last ten years rediscovered each other, and feuding neighbors were forced to witness each other's emotional distress and realize they weren't so different after all. A lot happens in small-town waiting rooms.

One mild spring evening Steve, a man in his fifties, came in dressed in full Harley Davidson gear with an eight-pound white poodle under his left arm. One of the dog's paws was wrapped tightly in the red bandana that should've been on Steve's head, judging from the way his hair was matted. The dog had a traditional poodle groom, with a lollipop tail and close crop along his back, but he had a four-inch tall, blue mohawk that began above his eyes and tapered off near his rhinestone collar.

"His name is Meatloaf" Steve said. "He cut his paw." For a poodle, Meatloaf was stoic as we delicately unwrapped the bandana to reveal a paw pad partially sloughed off and bleeding. Steve continued to hold him, his face knotting up and mouth furrowing with each fabric fold we pulled away. "He jumped off before I came to a complete stop..." his voice quavered, uncomfortably close to tears.

"Oh, this has an easy fix!" Aimes said gayly, looking at a lip of tissue that needed a few stitches and a bandage. Neither of us wanted to see Steve cry.

"Good, I thought maybe he'd need..." moisture sprung to Steve's eyes anyway.

The chimes on the front door rang as another unannounced visitor entered. I made sure Steve, Aimes, and Meatloaf had what they needed before sticking my head around the door to find a middle-aged man with a shih-tzu dog in his arms. It turned out to be acute diarrhea "on my wife's favorite bedspread" but nothing life threatening. As I started the man on paperwork, Steve came out of the room behind me.

"Hey Ted," Steve said, smiling to the new visitor as if we'd been expecting him. "You got Molly there? What's Molly in for? Did you give her bacon drippings again?"

Ted shot me a guilty look, having already answered that she hadn't eaten anything unusual, then to Steve "Yeah, her plumbing's off. You here with Meatloaf?"

"Yup. Puney's fine on his new meds, but Meatloaf here..." he looked over his shoulder to the door behind him where Aimes had him under anesthesia. "He's getting a tune-up. Didn't wear his boots on the last ride."

The two men chatted quietly for a while. *You make it to the speaker meeting on Saturday night? Jared still using that joke about Christopher Columbus? Amy's fine at Columbia. No, Pam isn't the secretary for Alateen this year.*

Aimes brought Meatloaf out with a blue bandage over the stitches she'd just finished and lay him on a folded blanket by Steve's feet to wake up from anesthesia, before turning to Molly. The chimes went off again as the door opened and we all looked up.

"Jake, hey man!" Molly's owner said brightly to the new face neither Aimes nor I recognized. Jake looked stricken. He was carrying a small terrier under his arm. "Dildo ate a bag of chocolate chips" he said tersely to everyone in the room.

"How long ago?" I asked, still without introductions.

"Twenty minutes".

Dildo had won a place at the front of the line and I turned to get a kennel set up for him and supplies to decontaminate his gut. I put on my soothing mantle of kindness when I returned to take the unfortunately named dog. "You did just the right thing," I assured Jake, "really, he should be just fine after he brings it back up."

Smiling, Steve attempted to add some jocularity "And Ted here was just about to do a tenth step after telling the nurse he hadn't given any people food to Molly! Weren't you Ted?"

Ted looked at me "It wasn't as much as I normally give; it shouldn't be her problem—".

I waved away his concerns. People either forgot or omitted useful information all the time. It was worst when pets had gotten into drugs or sex toys. I informed him a radiograph would be a good idea. He agreed and I reached to scoop Molly up.

"Meatloaf looks like he stayed past last call!" Ted suddenly noticed Steve's dog was bobbing his head from side-to-side and stumbling forward in a zigzagging attempt to stand. They laughed.

"Good thing he's neutered" Steve mumbled. More laughter.

I turned away with Molly. Aimes was already cleaning up chocolate vomit in the back kennel where Dildo was evacuating his stomach, as planned. The door chimed again and Paul, our chipper UPS driver entered with two large, brown boxes. He always kept our delivery until the end of his day, which the beginning of ours, around 7 p.m. He always wore short, brown, knee-length pants with his UPS uniform, giving him the air of an overgrown, graying British school boy.

Ted greeted him first "Paul! Let me help you with that!"

"It's just their pill vials and syringes, Teddy, really light stuff." But he handed off some boxes as if they did this together all the time. Paul quickly scanned the room, his face blooming with pleasant surprise. "Well now, if this isn't just the Buckeye men's meeting here…"

"Dildo ate chocolate. Molly has the shits and Meatloaf didn't wear the right gear to ride." Ted reported.

Steve nodded and indicated to Meatloaf, still bobbing his head "He's coming off his bender, at the moment."

Paul knew where the shipment went, so I continued on with paperwork and multi-tasking to care for the patients. The next thing I heard from the front room was Paul's solemn voice starting: *Who's father?* And then a powerful choral rumble, *Our father who art in heaven, hallowed be….*

They kept their impromptu AA meeting short. Paul's teenage son arrived with a large pizza about fifteen minutes later. By 10 p.m. all the pets were comfortable, if not bewildered, and ready to go home.

There were more jokes and backslapping. As Ted turned to go he said "Many thanks, young lady. You can now say you're a friend of Bill W. !"

"Was he here?" I asked earnestly. They chuckled.

"He was, in his way." Steve finished.

Aimes' clinic drew a pool of eclectic, creative and devoted employees the likes of which I've never seen anywhere else. It was a safe country inside that clinic, the land of misfit toys. Some of it was the nature of the town itself, a northern college town with rental cabins and communes, a town that drew those of us who don't always play by the rules. Off-duty employees might drop by at 2 a.m. to watch a movie or do their laundry. Employee meetings often started with reclamation of socks and underwear accidentally left behind. Every employee had a second or third vocation while working for Aimes: student, dog musher, heavy-equipment operator, LGBT advocate, hang glider, visual artist, goat milker, iguana rescuer, home builder, beekeeper, smoke jumper, writer. People who worked for Aimes were incapable of being boring. Yet being exciting incurs risks. The hang glider broke his leg, the goat milker wept when one of her girls died, the builder didn't get done on time and ended up living in a tent through a harsh winter (and then in the basement of Aimes' clinic). But someone was always there for you. One young employee was clearing some trees off some land she owned on a bright summer day. She didn't make it to work for one shift. Then she missed another shift. She had been killed by the electricity in an unexpected power line. She'd been pioneering on her acreage without plumbing, caring for sled dogs and other animals by hand-carrying 5-gallon jugs of water she picked up at the coin-operated dispenser on the edge of town. During the immediate aftermath of her death other employees from Aimes' clinic rushed to care for the animals by loading a truck with water containers and heading to the coin-op. Each of the two women on the trek thought the other had gotten enough change for the filling station. Between the two of them, they only had fifty cents.

Once they put the two quarters in, however, the dispenser never shut off. After getting 45 gallons of water and calling the water company's hotline to report the trouble, they had no choice but to drive away from the nozzle. They were forced to leave it on the ground where it was still pulsing out vigorous waves of icy fresh water in the dust.

interlude: drunk dogs and sidecars

It's changed now, but for the longest time the antidote for a dog that had ingested antifreeze poison within the preceding twelve hours was to get them drunk. Aimes' office manager of the emergency clinic used to go to the warehouse store and ask for the largest bottle of Everclear grain alcohol they had. She'd choose a variety of other products to muddle the story in the check-out line. Sometimes there was a genuine need for duct tape or pens, coffee and tampons. Often we were the beneficiaries of mega boxes of snack foods or human pain reliever. But the litany of drunk dogs is cemented in my memory. They were always massive dogs, never little poodles or yorkies. And the whole point of getting them really drunk was to make them dilute and urinate out the toxin, so all too frequently we had to escort swaying, stumbling dogs attached to fluid lines and leashes out into sub-zero temperatures and snow. In my memory, it's always January.

One last Vaudevillian memory from Aimes' clinic involves the technician with the WWII era motorbike with a sidecar. He often did what is called "the body run"—taking the deceased, frozen animals for cremation. There is actually an art to scheduling the body run, it's one part planning and one part magic. Every clinic has a set amount of freezer space. There are scheduled euthanasias and unscheduled euthanasias. Typically, crematoriums only accept bodies on certain days (because they only run their furnace on certain days) and each clinic pays a fee for cremation. The art is in knowing when to make the body run before you have to stash deceased animals in colder, out-of-the-way places in the clinic, which can precede disaster. I remember one technician scrambling under the counter looking for a tiny piece of dental equipment she'd dropped, when suddenly "Oh shit! Squeaker the guinea pig...!" She exclaimed, handing me a box that was slightly damp on the bottom. Another artistic component to planning the body run is loading your freezer appropriately. Do not... I repeat... Do NOT... put the

100-pound dog flat on the bottom of the freezer. I once attempted to lever up such a dog solidly adhered to the bottom of the freezer with a shovel. The shovel had dry rot in the handle, broke, and clocked me on the skull with such a loud cracking sound I was sent home for the rest of the day. But the technician with the motorbike sidecar, he had excellent intuition for the magic of the body run. He'd take into account full moons, holidays, and hunting season. He could pack a lot of frozen animals in that thing, cover them with a tarp so that no one idling along side him at the stop light would suspect the truth, and still be back at the clinic before Aimes could tell her poodle dog and vulva story for the 83rd time.

10

LOST AND FOUND

I t's a blasphemous comparison, but the only one that's true. The dog that looked at me through the cage bars that day had the eyes of a Buchenwald prisoner—incisive, wild, penetrating, rapacious. His red collar hung like a yoke on an ox. Two tiny silver bowls, just big enough for the tip of his muzzle, were in his kennel. Both were empty. One was turned over in frustration. He was an anatomy lesson. The wings of his hips pushed through his chocolate-colored coat and skin as if to flee the circumstance. His shoulders barely kept him upright. I could see the activity of the heart through the ribs on the right side. No disease did this. A disease process would've killed before getting to such a stage of emaciation. This was starvation. The tiny bowls were an effort to keep him from gorging himself to death with his own hunger. Feed small and frequent meals. Small and frequent and hope the digestive system could still do something with the food.

When on the later shift, I always started my day with a walk-through of the kennels. Pets' names would be on the whiteboard up front, but a clear picture of color, size and personality always helped to know what was happening. On that day I emerged from my kennel walk with the same stunned look most others wore in reaction to the dog.

"You saw him?" Julie asked. "That's Ned"

Ned was a name for a chubby Labrador with squeaky toys, not for the animal back in that kennel. "Yeah . . ." I answered, my questions implicit in my response. Julie didn't answer me for a few seconds. She was calculating drug doses. Then she started, "The reporter is up front with the cameraman. Do you want to be in the picture? Nobody else wants to do it."

"What's . . . ?" I started to ask, when a man stuck his head around the door into the treatment area, a bag hanging from his left arm and the tidy, inquisitive look of a reporter.

"Let's do this, ladies, who's my model?"

"Is it for the local paper?" I asked, still pointed towards Julie as she adjusted her glasses to read the fine lines on a tuberculin syringe.

The caffeinated reporter behind me chirped "It'll start local, we'll see where it goes. Don't be bashful, you look great!" He waved me over in a business-like way. He clearly had other stories to get to.

I went back into the kennel and put a slip-lead around Ned's neck and slowly led him out. There was the sense that he was present in the world, but released from it at the same time.

When we entered the treatment area the photographer visibly tried to contain his alarm at Ned's condition. Ned wasn't vibrating with exuberance the way normal Labradors do. He didn't need to be manipulated into position with the praise and the promise of biscuits. He sat on his blanket and stared, a wild, blank stare.

The photo was taken in front of a fireplace back in Vance's office, before their clinic was remodeled. I'm looking down at Ned wistfully, my slender arm extending from my oversized scrub top to place the flat of my palm on his ribcage. I was not yet 25. The Internet age was just beginning, and the term "viral' was still relegated to medicine.

I never met Ned's owner, or even talked to him on the phone, but I knew he was a photojournalist. I'd idolized Ansel Adams in my teens, thinking I might become a photographer myself. If I'd taken a different path that might've happened. The appeal of stories like Ned's generate from our ability to insert ourselves into the narrative. We fictionalize what we need to to uncork the relief we need.

The first time Ian pulled a camera up to his eyes in 1972 he felt waves of both relief and excitement. The world was enormous and enthralling, bubbling with verve and motion. The way his mother spoke of Grand Central Station in New York, five hours south, struck him as the way he experienced the world every day—overflowing, unraveling, gravid and often confused. The little window inside the camera framed a visual sentence, something with a beginning and an end; a flourish that was corralled and composed. By the time Ian was fifteen, photography was no longer a hobby but had become his vision. He could look and react with his own eyes, but he never saw anything until it came to him through the lens. There was never a question of vocation or college major for him. Sometimes he felt sadness for the way fate had chosen his career; sometimes he felt sadness for those who would never feel the same thing.

For many years Ian was content to work with the images in the nooks and crannies of East Coast living. Words like 'kaleidoscopic' and 'perfect discord' had flown out of critics' mouths when assessing his work. He married and had a baby girl. In the honeymoon phase after Annie's birth his photo subjects became even more intimate: tiny socks and shoes falling into sunlight, the particular way a pile of jarred spaghetti smeared across the table of a high chair. Ian was satisfied with this work. But, like light coming in underneath a door, he felt more and more drawn back to the outdoors, to tableaus of expanse, of vistas, and the extremes of small against large. His immediate response to this feeling, and to the fact that they now had a half-acre of fenced-in yard, was to get a dog. Why not have the whole picture? A young family, a new home, and a chocolate colored puppy that bounded towards them with his mouth open wide enough for a tennis ball, and paws big enough to knock Annie over and leave her laughing for long minutes and forgetting any pain in her fall. Annie named the pup. Ned.

In the autumn of 1997 he stood on the newly constructed deck of their home. He stood and looked south, keening his face through trees and houses as if he might see Florida through it all. One house had an inflatable Halloween spider hanging off the roof. A chimney had mineral streaks down its side from mortar left out in the elements. To his west would be the Atlantic Ocean. And to the northeast . . . to *his* north and east, would be Alaska. Even the word "Alaska"—the way it both started and ended with the open-lipped vowel 'a' lent an ephemeral, zephyrus quality. Since his father had given him a picture book about the Great State he'd wanted to make it a destination. He was not getting younger.

It took ten months to find a publisher that would give him enough advance to scrape together funds for travel and supplies. Ian's wife, Kathy, was initially thrilled with the idea. As the weeks went by however, as the project became more real. Their basement began filling with dried food, rainproof clothing, tripods and gloves. A faint air of apprehension entered their home. Their small town picked up the news and Ian agreed to be in the Fourth-of-July parade in the vehicle he'd chosen for the journey, a 1975 Toyota Truck, a vehicle old enough to have both personality and the element of risk. Ian would drive off after the barbeque that ended the parade.

Annie understood that daddy was going on an exciting trip. She picked up on the apprehension in her mother's comments and demeanor. She picked up on the level of fame her father was garnering. Even at age 6, she understood the trip was actually a journey, not a week in the woods with Uncle Joe.

"Daddy," Annie said one Sunday afternoon when her mother had created a purposeful comfort-food lunch of tomato soup and grilled cheese sandwiches "Take Ned".

Ian and Kathy spent the night gnawing on the psychology of their daughter: was she frightened? Did she feel left behind? Why was she offering up their dog as traveling companion? "She has a good idea . . ." Ian broached after Kathy ran out of reasons for Annie's comment.

"Marketing. You're thinking about marketing tactics again." Kathy said with disappointment.

"Sure. It's got the oldest travels-with-Charlie appeal." Ian again thought of Annie's tone-of-voice when she said 'Ned *wants* to go'. "And I think Annie would take some vicarious pleasure in having him with me."

The send-off at the 4th of July town parade was everything Ian imagined it would be. In one of his new leather-bound notebooks, chosen specifically for journaling. Ian later wrote how, only a century ago (a mere ten decades) a journey of this magnitude meant a willingness to never see your home town again. Ian imagined what it was like to read about the birth of a grandchild in a precious letter freighted via sternwheeler, steam engine, a leather satchel on the back of a horse. He could imagine what it was like to never meet that child until a letter in her own penmanship arrived six years later. Human beings needed that sense of nostalgic longing, some dream that always holds out and never completes. Mobility was a modern construct of plane and automobile and had, to some degree, left them all bereft. Everywhere, all at once, people were trying to find a new vehicle for their yearning now that the whole world was so accessible. His goal was to illuminate these things as best he could.

In the past, Ian had watched Ned dream. He would lie flat across the carpet, his front and rear legs spread apart to make two 'V' shapes stemming from his body. It would start with a slight stretch of his neck, a soft warble in his throat. The vocalizations would escalate into open-mouth yelps, dream-barks, and then a paddling of his legs. Ian had seen it enough to know it was not a seizure. Was he chasing rabbits, treeing bears? Was he running from something or running towards something? Ned had lived a sedate, suburban life with the exception of a few walks in the woods with Annie on weekends. Could he know a bear the same way a human knows a serpent, without ever seeing one?

The first few days of driving were heady. Ned had his head out the passenger window, the scenery opening up like a fist uncurling.

Bad coffee in disposable cups came from rest stops that served big, beasty men that lumbered into the paid shower kiosks. Ian would feel, many years later, that his most incisive images came from the topography of that first week. In those first days, especially when he nested into the chrysalis of his sleeping bag, he wondered what he had done and what he was doing, leaving his family in such a way. Ned, like a heat-seeking missile would always come over and lie on top of him. Ned didn't lie next to him or behind him or at his feet. Ned lay contentedly *on top* of him, as if Ian were a log he intended to anchor into the ground. Occasionally, Ned would let out a small, windy belch from his evening meal.

A photojournalist friend met Ian in Montana, just before he crossed into Canada, to take some of the images back to a safe place, exchange some of the broken equipment, and simply to check in. Ian was OK. He was OK, but he had become unable to pinpoint his emotions or really connect with what he was seeing. He didn't share that information, of course, but more and more Ian looked towards Ned to understand what was happening, what he was feeling, and how to live in the moment. Ned was unabashedly happy to visit with anybody. At night, he was vigilant, mildly afraid of every noise. When they stopped at diners, stores, and rest stops, Ned could barely pull away from the kind hands and words of strangers. When in open country, Ned sniffed close to the ground and urinated again and again, claiming intimacy with every rock and tree. These were the tight, minor places Ian found himself photographing.

Just before crossing into Canada Ian felt overcome with the desire to spend an evening in a motel. He had an urge to sleep off the ground on a mattress, to wake and shower, to click a button and revisit the inanity of television. His decision was so sudden he pulled off at the first anonymous motel sign he could find. An office flanked a short strip of rooms. Inside, an aged, wrinkled man reclined in a leather chair in front of a TV that didn't work, a white-muzzled golden retriever by his feet. He was reading a Louis L'Amour novel. His wife, her hairdo as round and motherly as her body, did the business transaction and gave Ian his key. "You travelin' alone, honey?" she asked with concern. Ian shared pertinent shreds of his story. "That's still a long road, baby," she responded. " If you didn't have your dog, I'd offer you Willy for the night." The old golden lifted his head at the sound of his name. In the morning the woman demanded he come into their kitchen for a full breakfast. Ian was stunned to hear his own voice almost quaver at her kindness.

The scenery changed. Ian and Ned entered the Yukon, the upper portion of the North American continent. Low steel-colored mountains under mackerel skies created an endless procession of voided days. Ned became the most vibrant thing to Ian in such a post-apocalyptic world. In his journal, Ian wrote about the darker trenches of dreamscapes, those that opened a great vault of terror. He mused over the idea that anyone had ever traversed these roads in the late 1800's, before packaged foods, the occasional gas station, and radio.

Alaska. They entered the state at the end of August, the destination shaped like an elephant head on the map. Customs was a square, grey-blue building in the middle of nowhere. Ian handed his driver's license to the woman. He answered her questions, realizing he'd spoken to no one but Ned in three solid days. They made it from Massachusetts to Alaska. Something inside Ian sighed and slouched. They were as good as there, the very top of the continent: Prudhoe Bay.

Ian was going to save most of the more tourist-oriented sightseeing until they were returning from their northward thrust. He'd likely sell the truck in Anchorage and fly home. They were entering the month of September; margins of safety with the weather were narrowing. They were 400 miles to the finish, and Ian was ready. It seemed that Ned was, too.

At 2 p.m. on September 3rd Ian spotted a three-quarter-ton truck towing a small boat just ahead of him. He slowed from their comfortable traveling speed of 50 miles-per-hour to 30 to follow it. The vehicle's speed continued to decrease and Ian watched it swerve to the shoulder and stop. He slowed down and parked behind it.

A slim, red-haired man emerged from the cab, lurching towards one of the truck's rear tires before ever making eye contact with Ian. "Fucking Flat." Then the young man straightened himself and acknowledged Ian "Sorry, to slow you down, man." Ned was suddenly alongside them; Ian hadn't closed the door to the cab. "Nice, dog." The man stroked Ned's ears.

After they'd unhitched the trailer carrying the boat, Ian stood holding lug nuts in his hand while the man changed the tire. Ned was around somewhere, marking the wild terrain with a scent that would surely baffle the wildlife. They exchanged their stories about how long they'd been in Alaska, their goals and families. They'd just begun to lower the jack under the truck.

It happened so fast. Neither man registered the approach of a semi. It was the kind of truck that gave the 'Haul Road' they were on its name. It was the sudden, onerous, pleading sound of its horn that made Ian swivel around, just in time to notice a chocolate-colored slur of movement in front of the truck's massive grill. The behemoth sped on, Ian's heart hanging above his sickened abdomen, and once the truck cleared his vision in its unconcerned hurry, he saw only the tiniest flash of Ned, disappearing into the brush on the other side of the road. Ned didn't answer his calls. For days that turned into weeks, Ned didn't answer when Ian called his name.

I know it was Beth who first met Ned at the animal shelter. She was the early-shift shelter worker in the town at that time. I like to imagine her keying the door on that crisp October day, the shelter lobby decorated the paper pumpkins and harvest colors. The morning sound and smell of a kennel are chaotic and disorienting, sometimes overwhelming with animal mess from the night before. Still, the first one in had to start the computers, set up paperwork and check the overnight drop-off cages, the kennels that opened to the outside so anyone wanting to anonymously rid themselves of a pet or drop off a nuisance animal could do so. Sometimes there were yowling mother cats and kittens, sometimes a dead dog. On Monday, October 18th, 1999, Beth opened the kennel door on Ned. The dog should not have been able to stand, and his back leg was scabbed and swollen. A note was duct-taped to his collar "found mile 23 Elliot Highway". It was twenty miles from where Ian had last seen him. Ned's tags announced his name and provided a Massachusetts phone number. Beth thought that was odd, but she dialed anyway.

"Save him" was the directive from the owner in Massachusetts. He gave his credit card number. Geoff from animal control brought Ned to the clinic late that afternoon, after I'd left for the day. Ned's leg wound had been easy to clean and dress. The day after the newspaper article came out, however, donations and support came pouring in. An airline company donated his plane ticket home. A local pet store donated a crate for his travel.

What amazed me was that, within three days of carefully metered feedings, the wild-thing look in Ned's eyes went away. The aggressive need of the concentration camp victim disappeared. It was subtle, and profound. Yet his air of distance and reserve never changed. It was strange to work with a Labrador of such self-contained deportment—pride, it seemed at times. Ned stayed with us for a week. He ate, he drank, he slept, and he went for walks. And then he was gone. Geoff from animal control picked him up in the off-hours, leaving a kennel with a blanket and an open door when I arrived for my shift. I felt a pang at his disappearance, a tinge of dismay at not knowing his future and letting him go. I can only imagine what his owner felt. He told someone that he'd camped beside the road for almost ten days before deciding it was time to leave. He felt unable to carry on with the final leg of his trip that would complete his photojournalism project and returned home prematurely.

Perhaps we humans find so much inspiration in our animals because they lay bare who we wish to be. Cats that go back into burning buildings to retrieve their kittens are the penultimate example of loyalty and self-sacrifice. Pet birds escape and are found on the other side of the continent, exemplifying a need for freedom. A small tortoise wanders out of a suburban yard and is then found in the downtown area. We are curious. Puppies are trapped inside the walls of a home under construction and a dozen men sacrifice thousands of dollars pulling apart their work to save them. We are heroes. In our animals we find what we feel we've lost.

11

STUFF & NONSENSE

There is whimsy in the pet supply industry. You've seen it pet outfits, toys, beds and food. The little pouches of fish-shaped 'Beachside Crunch' party snacks for cats, the bacon look-alikes made from compressed cow lips and soy with the wide-eyed, open-mouthed cartoon dog of happiness on the package, these are the resultant words and images of carefully employed psychologists and focus groups. None of it is haphazard; all of it is backed by research. The pet supply industry is almost completely recession proof; we cannot back away from cute. As a young technician spoiled by many walks through pet stores, I once asked a marketing salesman for Hill's prescription pet food why they'd settled on an un-cute logo of a red rectangle sitting next to a blue rectangle. It seemed to take great effort for him to reach into his memory for an answer. "Well, I think somebody did a study that said people buy more with strong, primary colors. And the medical thing . . . it has more authority with just the blocks." He's right; products without cartoons on them are more expensive.

Veterinary hospitals need a lot of stuff. A brand-new practice owner summed it up best the day she went stomping across the treatment area muttering "I didn't know you needed a contract with an oxygen company to buy air!" Sure, we need oxygen tanks and beeping monitors and new washing machines, but we also need an unending supply of antibiotics, prescription food, latex gloves and cotton-tipped applicators. At one clinic we had a 'Whine List' for out-of-stock inventory items. Beyond the basics, there were things we needed that we didn't know we needed: green chew bones with plant hormones that cleaned a dog's teeth, button-shaped, chicken-flavored putty you could wrap around a pet's pill, food additives that would prevent tear-staining in the corners of a white-dog's eyes. And for all these products we needed salesmen. Companies manage their products regionally, so we see the salesman again and again. They are sincere. They believe you need what they have to sell. They move through their visits and phone calls with a beguiling naiveté, an arrow-straight commitment to their path. If dumped in the middle of a veterinary emergency they would be the ones paralyzed by their options.

One more adaptive quality of such salesman is their ability to stay poised and positive amidst detractors. A Eukanuba representative once came to a clinic where I worked with a wonderful young military wife whose husband was deployed. The salesman had us seated in our break-room, his computer slideshow illustrating the bioavailability of his food's nutrients through an animation of twinkling squares and diamonds. When he was sure someone was about to start snoring, he began putting sample bags of food out for display, the tried-and-true varieties as well as two new ones. His head and torso emerged from under the table holding a glossy bag of the formula he unveiled at this last visit "Multi-Cat". This food was somehow magically created to be all things to all cats, and taste good at the same time. As soon as she saw the glint of the fluorescent lights on the bag Theresa blurted "I send those samples to my husband and, you know, the Iraqi cats won't even eat that stuff!"

Not an eyebrow lift or pause from our food representative "Our food is in Iraq?! Can you get some pictures?!"

Mike was a sales representative who serviced a region encompassing 4000 miles. Over the years, as I moved from clinic to clinic, city to city, Mike and I kept finding each other. When he caught sight of me at the third clinic, a breathy, amazed and curious "You—" escaped his mouth. "I almost forget what clinic I'm and what city I'm in when I see you!" He exclaimed. I'd gather news from him about old friends from different cities, who'd left what clinic, who was on the state medical board or was retiring. The question of my mobility always hung in the air, but over the years we began to feel an unspoken kinship in our vagrancy. Mike was a figure straight from a 1950's sitcom, a throwback to a time when people chose their professions and the age of 22 and retired from the same employer. He had a solid, square, clean-shaven face with dark brown hair. His suits never had a wrinkle and fit perfectly. At one clinic, we used to dare each other to touch him and see if the fabric crinkled like a cat toy. On his business card he sat as if it were a tenth-grade photo, face directly to the camera against a light-blue background, shoulders and torso barely angled as if you'd suddenly caught his attention. He was the regional pharmaceutical rep for a large company. His voice inflected at the end of his sentences. He was always surprised and brightened when we took the time to speak with him.

The beautiful thing about the drug companies is they have lots of money to give the veterinary staff free stuff. Dr. Vance was proud of the fact that their clinic had sold enough carprofen to be awarded not one, but three cube refrigerators. Instead of the requisite 'Maytag' or 'Whirlpool' in the upper left, each bore the name of the arthritis medication that had purchased the appliance in the first place. Mike (and others like him) were endowed with money to purchase the entire veterinary clinic lunch on the days he came to unveil new medications and products. The office manager would collect the orders for Chinese food or pizza or sandwiches and fax it to Mike, who'd end up making three trips into the break room to unload the banquet feast. He loved this part of his job. Of course, problems with particular products also landed under his jurisdiction. A more esoteric product we used was a powder we mixed with a liquid to make a hardening compound that we infused into a dog's anal glands before surgically removing them. Even stranger than our need for such a compound was the fact that the powder component was shipped by air but, due to the "volatile nature" of the liquid, that component had to come by barge. Six weeks could go by while we waited for the second-half of the mixture. It's like waiting a month for the spoon to your soup. Like most quirky exceptions, the lesson was learned the hard way—with a scheduled surgery and a shipment that was due to arrive after the fact. Poor Mike's voicemail was regaled by the increasingly desperate and irritated messages from technicians as the surgery deadline approached. Then the office manager came back at 10 a.m. on a Friday.

"Mike's in town today. He wants to know what we want for lunch."

It was the older, big-bosomed technician who'd been responsible for grappling with the issue of the missing "volatile liquid" who loudled mumbled, "Fuckin' peal-and-eat shrimp!" as she heisted a large molar out of the jaw of an anesthetized bulldog.

Mike came skipping in with platter after platter of shrimp, his eyes gleaming and a cheerful smile on his lips. He also brought us the product that had caused so much tension. "I'm so embarrassed for our company!" he said, as he handed it to the technician who'd demanded shrimp. Taking anger out on Mike would've been like savaging a boy scout. We began calling him "Mike and the shrimp barge" that day, and the name stuck for many years. He wore his surprised, impish grin as we continued to joke it would be a good name for his rock n' roll band. "I'm on it!" He'd always say. "The debut recording is in the mail!"

Almost 99% of veterinary drugs come from the human pharmaceutical industry. Companion animals often metabolize the drugs differently than humans, and drugs are used for different purposes, so please do not start medicating your own pet, *but* BigPharma Animal Health and its human counterpart are barely separate entities. The release of new drugs on the human side has just as much relevance to those of us watching with dog biscuits in our hands. No one, however, had to work in a medical field to get caught up in the humor that came with the release of Pfizer's Viagra, the drug that made baby boomers good dancers, the drug that spawned hours of puns and pseudonyms. Mydixadrupin, Ibepokin. Pfizer's Riser. When the first blush of humor wore off Viagra it then became the subject of feminist essays and insurance discussions. The publicity was everywhere. And poor, pure-hearted Mike wore the cloud of association to every clinic he visited. Later, Viagra would find use in the veterinary field as a cardiac drug, but while the rest of the world was suddenly besieged by the phrase 'erectile dysfunction' and could speak of nothing else, Mike was tasked with marketing a new, non-funny antibiotic to the different clinics he served.

I was at Dr. Vance's clinic at the time. Dr. Vance's office manager, Skip, was 6'4" and 250 pounds. He had blond hair and blue eyes and the emotional maturity of anyone's 14-year-old brother. Poop jokes were his specialty. He had a Shakira doll on his desk and a poster of Britney Spears on the wall above the fax. Associate veterinarians knew he was impossible to work with if you didn't share his political affiliation. His comments about women always grazed the mark of sexist, metering just under 'harassment' but neutralized by his willingness to take rude comments about men in return.

"What do you want Mike to bring for lunch?" Skip asked us.

Skip let us bumble out ideas about Thai food or pizza (we all knew enough not to ask for shrimp again) before saying "I was thinking about bun-length hot dogs!"

I don't think he actually expected us to laugh that time, but he did take pleasure in our eye-rolling.

As it was, our buddy Mike showed up with several foot-long deli sandwiches, each with a petticoat of lettuce and unzipped into diagonal strips for our picnic. Random commentary about the heavy crust on the bread and the thickness of the meat inside elicited an expression of pleased boredom, acceptance, and delicate detachment from Mike.

"You'll really like this antibiotic! It has once-daily dosing and gets the job done in less than ten days!" He began. We were still pulling sodas from their six-pack webbing and making sure we'd grabbed one napkin, not six, to go with our pieces of sandwich.

Mike was capable of small talk until he opened his marketing materials. Once he'd seen the glimmer of his shiny packages, however, he was constitutionally unable to talk about anything beyond the product. He truly had a passion for what he did. "In the next few years we expect to be able to have this drug in injectable form. For cats, one injection would last for ten days, meaning no more pills!"

We technicians stopped mid-mouthful at the prospect. Mike responded to the sound of our awe with a bashful "It's still a while away, but it's coming!"

"Tease." Bethany stated.

Almost every clinic has one—the woman in charge of inappropriate comments. Some are better at it than others, but they hone their identity on it. Bethany knew she'd arrived in the role when the whiteboard with the non-medical supply needs listed 'floor stripper' and Skip had drawn an arrow to the product and written 'Bethany'. While I never managed to be as verbally irreverent, I was about to discover a proclivity for innuendo that would haunt me for a long time.

"Now, I'm handing out some brochures . . ." Mike slid each of us an 8x11 glossy, paperboard trifold off a stack from his briefcase. It was a promo material that wasn't easily lost. The computer presentations were nice, but as active veterinary workers we didn't have much time to be on the computer. We'd watch the show and forget. At times it seemed we are the last of the 'face time' work era; on our feet, on the phone, running about with syringes and bandage scissors, resistant to the most basic tenets of Excel programming. But a shiny foldout like those at a car dealer had staying power. They were just fancy enough that you wouldn't feel right about throwing them out.

In a unified flurry of motion we opened our material. Running her thumb along the laminated inside page, Bethany mumbled "We can even get these things wet".

Mike plunged in. "So on that first page you can see the bar graph of the efficacy. 98% of dogs over eight weeks of age responded to a ten-week course of treatment for mixed aural, and dermal infections. 82% responded to urinary and perirectal infections of anal glands . . .".

"Is this clinically or on culture with MIC?"

Just as every clinic has a woman with inappropriate comebacks, every clinic has a skeptic nerd. Still, I was impressed how Mike had mastered the medical vocabulary necessary for this. It hadn't always been that way, I sensed that he'd been practicing.

"I think this is clinically." He looked at the bottom of the page, scanning the asterisks and tiny t-shaped addendums. "Well wait, this has the MIC results, but they are slightly lower."

This type of exchange went on for a while including how the method of action was different than that of the cephalosporins (which still sound like aliens to me, despite being a very common class of antibiotics), why nervous-system build-up was not a problem in pets, tissue distribution and total body clearance. As technicians, the more we understood this, the more authority we had when answering client questions. Sometimes our veterinarians forgot some of the details, giving us a chance to impress them with our powers of retention. But we technicians typically sat there wondering if the pill would have bitter residue when shoving it down a pet's throat, what it would cost and how much to charge clients, and if you could half and quarter the tablets without having them turn into dusty crumbles. Over the years marketing companies have opened their eyes to the fact that technicians make the bulk of purchasing decisions in the field.

I have the attention span of the average ninth-grader. When sitting down I twitch my leg or play with my hair. I always read ahead, and for this, in this situation, it made for trouble.

On the back of the tri-fold was a picture of the tablet itself. Pfizer chose to take up almost the entire length of the page with the tablet. There was a full ten-inches of pill perfectly balanced on one of its rounded ends. It was also just the right phallic color, an ambiguous human skin tone with a sincere blush. No explanation accompanied the photograph, just the simple, solid, image of the pill with its brand name running its length and the distinct logo on the bottom right.

Yes, these handouts were meant to sit on someone's desk until everyone decided the clinic needed to order and use the new drug. It would stand out from all the other paperwork. Yes, we technicians could clearly the see the tablet was scored in the center, so our concern with modifying the dose for smaller pets was addressed. But, in my mind, there was simply no way BigPharma could've chosen the design without the deliberate intent of tapping into the media splash happening with Viagra.

"Mike . . ." I started with a questioning tone. As soon as I'd opened my mouth to remark on the back page I thought better of it. Mild, innocent Mike shouldn't have to be backed into a corner to confirm my suspicions. The business of marketing was not his business. He was the conduit. I corrected my inquiry. "I see the scoring to half the tablets, but can you quarter them?"

"I think the different strengths the drug comes in are meant to cover those contingencies. You shouldn't have to."

I was waiting for Bethany to say something, maybe even Skip. I simply could not be the only one seeing the image and not reflecting on it. But no one said a word.

The visit with Mike ended with someone making an afternoon pot of coffee. The expensive phrase for the after-lunch slump was borrowed from noticing what happens to a snake after it's just swallowed a whole rabbit: "postprandial torpor". But the phones were ringing and the next appointment had been waiting in the lobby for fifteen minutes. I hung back to get some fresh coffee. Even after everyone rose to move on, not a word was said about the back-page ten inches. I had to take action.

Surreptitiously, in the bathroom, I took scissors and stream-lined the antibiotic's silhouette to let its true meaning emerge. My first attempt looked a little too much like a handgun, so I had to destroy a second information flyer . When I was satisfied with my handiwork I taped it to the vanity mirror in the employee bath-room and waited.

I waited all afternoon. No one said a word, not even Bethany. Was something wrong with me? Was my vision so warped or my stretch of abstinence so long that cutting phallus outlines from Mike's materials was simply viewed with tender pity? At the end of my work day I went to use the restroom and found my cut-out was gone. Neither Skip, Bethany nor anyone else had a history of suddenly becoming arbiters of humor standards. Like a graying sky, I was infused with shame. Walking by the trash cans on my way out of the treatment area towards where I kept my coat and bag, I glanced inside each can but saw no sign of my snubbed attempt at entertainment.

It was midwinter, the time of uninspired dark evenings taken up with a few errands to the store but not much more than keeping up with the basics of life. I had a long, black wool coat to keep the draft from my legs. Wearing scrub pants into the cold is never any fun. I was lucky that my car started; it'd been deeply cold for several weeks and everyone's vehicles had begun to snap belts and smoke and refuse. Still in a haze from a long day with pets and clients, coupled with my missteps in interpreting my co-workers, I drifted through the aisles of the grocery store, the mailboxes at the post-office. I was chilled enough that I even began water boiling for my pasta before I took off my coat. I draped it over the back of a chair by the door.

It was then that I saw the flash of color. Heat rose in my gut. I raised my coat in front of me and let its full length unfurl. There, on the back, in the middle, was the cut-out penis. I had driven, shopped, and picked up my mail with it taped to the back of my black wool coat.

"But you always notice things!" Skip demanded the next morning when I told him how his prank had played out. "What was *wrong* with you?"

"Blaming the victim, Skip. Never works." I said.

"Think of this as the start of a second career..." his voice dissolved in a gurgle of laughter, before he finished "It didn't specify a price, so maybe you could barter for your rent...".

Had Skip not been another clinic employee's husband and a general buffoon, he would've been the first person I ever punched. The next time the bank officer assigned to our clinic came to consult Skip about something official and important, Skip failed to notice that his Shakira doll was on her back, pink plastic legs in a wide, V-position, with her platform performance shoes still on.

For several weeks after that I was hypervigilant in the public places around town, examining faces and body language for signals that they recognized me as the penis girl. I was, at that time in my mid-twenties, still very much a self-conscious girl.

Mike came back a few weeks later just to check in and take an order. "Mike," I started with an air of conspiracy that frightened him a little. "We really enjoyed the info on the antibiotic last time . . .". His eyebrows still rode high on his forehead waiting for my disclosure. "I . . . uh . . . vandalized the picture on the back of that flyer . . . you know the—".

"You aren't the first one to do that."

"I'm not?!"

"Oh, no." He was matter-of-fact, but offered no details. I desperately wanted to hear about the kindred souls that made the same mistake..

I continued "Well, you know how Skip can be . . . a . . .".

". . . dork?"

"Yes!" We were really rolling in authentic communication now. I was pleased. "He stuck it on the back of my coat and I went to the grocery store and post office before I noticed!"

Mike's face opened in alarm and his brow furrowed in suitable indignation on my behalf. By then, however, the offense had softened and I was also willing to see the humor. Mike didn't laugh, but glistened as he said "You actually are the first person to have *that* experience with the promo materials."

A couple weeks later a little brown package arrived at the clinic for me. It was a cassette tape. Most of the world had switched to CDs but some of us still had cassette players in our cars and at home. The cassette was labelled "Mike and the Shrimp Barge: demo". A handwritten note on BigPharma stationary was enclosed: *Here is something from me and Mike Junior. I hope you enjoy it. Sincerely, Mike and the band*

I smuggled it home and played it there first, before bringing it back in for everyone to hear. Mike's son was probably four or five years old. He stumbled through an Elvis Presley song about shrimp, and then he did a bang-up job of reproducing the song from a 1965 commercial.

> *I wish I were an Oscar Mayer Weiner*
> *That is what I truly wish to be*
> *Cause if I were a oscar mayer weiner*
> *Everyone would be in love*
> *Oh everyone would be in love*
> *Everyone would be in love with me*

interlude: planning for the unplanned

Some animals are just angry. Sweet words, biscuits, getting them away from the owner they're protecting, none of these techniques will work. I avoid binary thinking, but I will say that when a client's dog is angry in your clinic there are two types of owners: the ones that will laugh while their dog gives you the scare of your life, and the ones that arrive carrying their own muzzle because they know there's going to be a problem. One afternoon a handsome German shepherd named Max came in for an eye exam. (Have I mentioned that 80% of aggressive dogs come in for some issue on their *face*?) I walked in and took a history from Max's owner, a diminutive, clean-cut man in his thirties or forties. Max growled the entire time. He was wearing a correctly-sized cloth muzzle that prevented him from opening his jaw but didn't impede breathing. Poor Max was truly amped up, his eyes wide, his constrained cheeks puffing out with his attempts to bark, small collections of white spittle-foam gathering around the muzzle. I didn't get a heart rate or temperature. His breaths-per-minute were clearly visible.

I took Max's chart into the doctor's office where the two afternoon docs were finishing lunch and emails. "Cherry eye recheck. This dog is a total handful…".

Dr. Meeks said "Oh! This is the dog that got Ginny pregnant!"

Ginny had been a dedicated young co-worker who embraced her unplanned pregnancy as best she could, finally moving several states away to be with her parents. We missed her. She was brilliant at paying attention to the details of inventory and talented in many other aspects. Meeks explained the flow chart of events. Ginny was bitten by Max seriously enough to go to the doctor and get antibiotics. Antibiotics messed up the efficacy of her birth control right as she got back together with her ex. Meeks finished with a humorous flourish "I need a tech who isn't likely to get within ten feet of a penis after working with this dog."

"How about within ten feet of a *non*-working penis?" I asked, since I had access to one in my life at the time.

"If you are absolutely certain it doesn't work, then come with me . . .".

12

FEAR FACTOR

I'm finding that, as I get older, the only really interesting people are those who go crazy at least once. I don't mean whooping it up on the town, or a bad day of yelling, I mean the kind of crazy people disclose to others in low-volumed voices. It would be much more convenient if we could predict *when* we were going to visit Crazytown (if only to pack a lunch because the food is really bad in there), but rest assured, once you've gone you are simply more qualified to be part of the human race.

When I met Victor Sprigg he was a veterinarian in his mid-fifties. He had a soft, jowly face. There was a plumpness in his whole body, a smooth-skinned softness that entertained the concept that Sprigg was a giant human infant. Most conjecture hovered around the idea that he had higher estrogen levels than most men. While this went unconfirmed, there was no argument that he'd fathered two daughters with an ex-wife who was "a blood-sucking louse".

I'd just started at a clinic where Sprigg worked part-time. It was a Tuesday afternoon. I was in the treatment area assembling an IV fluid line. The young assistant with a conspicuous hickey on her neck was folding surgical gowns and discussing movies. "I finally saw American Pie, the one where the boys are trying to lose their virginity before high school ends . . .".

"Yeah," I said with an eye-rolling tone of voice, watching the last bubble pass out the end of the IV line into the sink, "I heard about that one."

The mother of three sons asked "Is that the one where the kid sticks his dick in an apple pie?"

Dr. Sprigg's face jolted up from microscope. "I love that one!" You could hear the clang of a bell, a strange metallic silence in the air. His eyes wide with excitement, he proceeded to regale us with the entire plot of American Pie (which he'd seen three times) and tell us when the sequel would be released to video.

When Sprigg was not at our clinic he functioned as one of the town's only equine veterinarians. Horses don't whelp whole litters of puppies, or enjoy the same fecund speed of cat multiplication. They tend to birth a single, valuable foal after a lengthy gestation. For this reason, much of equine medicine is about fertility. Dr. Sprigg's affinity for a movie about a young man having sex with bakery products likely stemmed from his many years of quality time with horse vulvas. At one point we ordered him a small, heated, teeter-totter device that did something to preserve the sperm count in horse ejaculate. He accidentally dropped a vial and was scrambling to suck up the remainder with a syringe when he cried "The semen are jumping ship! We need life rafts!"

Other times Sprigg hadn't a clue about his humor. He was spaying a cat one morning when he kept sighing heavily and seemed quite sluggish. I asked if he was feeling well and he sighed again, replying "The semen came at midnight." The veterinarian a few feet away spewed her coffee all over her charts. Sprigg was, of course, referring to the imported stuff that arrived at the airport on dry ice.

Sprigg also seemed to enjoy telling us things that didn't inspire confidence. He'd tell us about his Xanax prescription, the time he grabbed the wrong tabby cat from a kennel and proceeded to instruct the owners how to give the insulin to their newly diagnosed diabetic cat, who promptly had a hypoglycemic seizure because it wasn't diabetic. Things happened to Sprigg that didn't happen to other people. He once reached to take a Chihuahua from a young woman's arms and his watch band caught in the knit of her fitted sweater. He was awkward and bashful with women in general, but with his hands tangled so near her breasts he panicked. Sprigg's strangled cries for help from the exam room were so tinged with terror the office manager thought Sprigg was having a heart attack and he used his shoulder to bust open the door. Another example involves ketamine, a drug commonly used in horses as a sedative. Some collusion of events during one of Sprigg's house calls left a syringe of ketamine, with the needle exposed, on the driver's seat of his truck. He sat on the drug, drove to the emergency room and got as far as the parking lot before having a good, long, drugged, amnesic snooze. And Sprigg's stories about the death throes of his marriage entered the unreal—food poisonings, hair pulling, drained fuel tanks and missing furniture. Despite the stories he had to tell, Sprigg always seemed as if he enjoyed reading the comic strip that was his life.

Regardless of how well you know your co-workers during your working hours, however, nothing can compare with spending several days together engrossed in professional development. That was the year I ended up driving the three-hundred miles to the state veterinary conference with a co-worker named Jane, who had an encyclopedic knowledge of country music. I sat back and let her mess around with the cassette player, enriching my listening experience with the biographical trivia of the singers. We stopped only once in seven hours, so by the time we arrived at the conference I was plagued by the sensations of chronic motion and a strong desire for barbecue.

The hotel lobby was a hive of activity with people just like us, veterinary professionals from around the state slinging luggage over their shoulders, cheerfully greeting old classmates, rifling through their conference packets to be sure their nametag was spelled correctly and they had the appropriate number of raffle tickets. Once Jane and I had checked in, our other co-workers Dr. Morris, and Dr.

Day beckoned us over to where they'd sprawled in large armchairs by the faux fireplace.

"Look at this!" Day exclaimed, waving a remote control device. She pointed it at the fireplace and began hitting buttons. The "flames" went from taking up the whole hearth, to minimizing by two gradients. "Look at these buttons for high-medium-low!" Meghan Day was a pretty young woman. She was entering her second year of marriage and finishing her first trimester of pregnancy.

"Once she breaks the fireplace we're left with car camping, which she won't enjoy in her condition." Christy Morris said. She was just over forty, with fine lines on her forehead from time in the sun bicycling and rock climbing.

Day protested "No one says in *your condition* anymore, Chris."

They'd clearly had several hours together to limber up. "OK! Preggo, Preggers, knocked up...". Morris turned to us "What room are you guys in?"

Jane looked at her keycard "402".

"Ha! We're in 403," then to Day, "I told you they'd line us up like this!" She turned back to us "If I snore you ladies can pound on the wall. And Sprigg is in 404."

"I know *he* snores" Jane said. "The whole fourth floor will probably hear."

"*You* snore?" Day asked Morris.

"I only snore after the third glass of red wine."

"Where's Sprigg?" I asked.

"Bathroom. He's been there for twenty minutes." Day replied.

When Sprigg came back from the restroom he had his usual jocular smile.

"We thought you'd climbed out a window and were heading for the hills!" Morris said.

"No chance, wouldn't miss the insemination lecture for the world." We all smiled. "But I'm not impressed with my room. Last year's was better."

"They should hold it at the hot springs every year." Day said.

"Just without the alcohol" added Morris, mischieviously.

"Huh? What happened?" Jane was interested.

Day rolled her eyes and began tucking her conference paperwork into her shoulder bag "My lips are sealed."

"Old Sprigg here—" Morris started with a broad smile.

"Oh, don't start THAT again, Christina!" Sprigg objected.

"Well why not?" She joked. "I could get you on sexual harassment!"

"Because you're gay!" Sprigg said.

"And that means there's no possible way you stole my swimsuit in a de-pantsing prank . . . ?!" She retorted.

"I can't hold my breath that long underwater to get your bikini bottoms off!" Sprigg protested, "I. did. not. do. it." He finished firmly and began to turn away.

"You *didn't*—"Jane said, looking from Morris to Sprigg.

Sprigg turned back and blurted "I didn't take them off! Someone was pulling a prank in the outdoor pool." Then to Morris "You shouldn't've been wearing a bikini—you were at a veterinary conference!"

Amidst the teasing my eye caught sight of a white fluttering off the back of Sprigg's belt. I leaned over to see more. I blinked and thought *no one does that, at least not in real life.* But it was true. I had to say something.

"Sprigg, you've got toilet paper hanging out of your pants."

Then, like a dog chasing its tail in silent frenzy, he spun around two times before grabbing the streamer of toilet tissue out of his trousers.

The conference proceeded with the clinking of ice in water glasses and spoons in coffee cups, eager drug and equipment reps with free pens and candy, and bits of useful information scribbled in the corners of our compendiums. Things didn't get interesting again until the dinner and raffle that night. After everyone had greeted old classmates and teachers, after Dr. Day had won a new stethoscope in the raffle, we all ended back at one circular table.

"I've always like the idea of doing epidurals on ortho cases, but—damn—it frightens me." Day said, after rehashing the pain-management lecture.

"I've always been afraid of clowns, myself." I added.

"Breast milk." Morris said flatly, pointedly looking away from Dr. Day.

"What?!"

"Just . . . maybe don't keep those little bottles in the lunch fridge after the baby comes, OK?"

Sprigg chuckled to himself. The four of us subconsciously had left a pause for him to say something. Nothing came. I turned to Day, "What's your biggest fear?"

"My *biggest* fear? Before or after getting pregnant?"

"Before."

Her face became thoughtful and serious. "I'm afraid of turning on my dryer with my cat inside. When I was a kid I did that on the way out to the school bus and our kitten was inside.

We stopped to take that in, imagining the gut-wrenching discovery of a tiny, warm, limp body, also sensing the group humor that'd we all used to deflect genuine intimacy had begun to crack.

"'That's awful!" Jane finally said for us, amidst our nodding. She went on "I had hamsters growing up, starting when I was about four, but they only live—"

"—like two years?" I finished.

Jane confirmed "Yeah, so my dad made sure he always got a picture of me holding the new hamster. Some dads want to measure your growth on a doorframe in the house. . nooo, my dad wanted a succession of photos of me holding a rodent. And one year we got this new one. I think I was about eleven, maybe twelve."

"When did this hamster tradition end?" Sprigg asked.

"When I left home."

"Good God!" he said.

". . . but that time when I was twelve, the hamster died the night we brought it home, but my dad *insisted* on a picture with it."

"Are you *serious?*" Day said, to underscore the horror, not in any hope Jane was joking.

"Yup. It was already in rigor. He made me stand under this willow tree in our yard like I did for all the other pictures."

"And that's why you you're afraid of pocket pets."

"I'm not *afraid,* I just don't like them. And I don't much like willow trees either."

Our conversation came to a rest. I sensed there was some untapped anecdote or jewel in Sprigg's mind. "Well, Dr. Sprigg, what is your big fear?" I asked.

He shifted in his seat, pushed his spoon against a tiny island of chocolate cake left on his plate. He told us in a soft, sincere voice, something so outrageous we were left considering there were infinite facets to him that we'd not yet seen.

We returned from the conference and settled into the rhythm of autumn. In climates like ours, with severe winter weather and deep-freezing temperatures, pumpkins, paper turkeys and pilgrim outfits entered the stores at the same time thousands of pounds of cat litter for road traction, dehydrated food and kerosene heaters went on sale, lending a festive, Cold War era feel to shopping. By Thanksgiving, Dr. Day was getting very round with her pregnancy and the temperatures were staying below zero. Around that time we finally got to meet Dr. Sprigg's personal pets, the creatures who'd become the lynchpin in his divorce settlement, a pair of Pekingese dogs his ex-wife had ordered from a breeder eight years earlier. Sprigg was required to take the dogs or his soon-to-be ex-wife wouldn't sign the divorce papers. The dog's names were "Maiden" and "China".

"That just about summed up our marriage" Sprigg explained. "Doris like novelty, spending money, and demeaning things."

"Maiden" was the female. She was blonde, and she was evil. "China" was the black male, and barely any nicer. Sprigg had brought them in with their hair matted into a thick-wooled pelt, causing skin irritation in several places. Their nails curled around into little moon-shaped cleats, a few of them growing all the way back around into the pads.

You could tell from the odor of their heads they had yeast infections in their ears. But every time you got within ten inches of them, their unkempt, smelly bodies would quake with their growling. Move in any closer, and their gray-green teeth would emerge from under their curled lips, occasionally making a lightening-fast lunging bite into the air. "You've heard of the cobbler's children having no shoes," Sprigg explained "and I'm so ashamed to be a vet and have dogs like this, but I know it's meant to be my wife's enduring punishment for me."

We ended up sedating "Maiden" and "China" to clean them up, instill ear medication and trim nails. The whole time Sprigg just stood there, stricken, mumbling about how Doris would kill him if the dogs died under anesthesia. The true horror of his entrapment with this woman was finally hammered home to us. In addition to all the other sacrifices, he'd given her the house in town and was then living on a large acreage in a cabin without plumbing. We'd seen pictures. It did have a Walden-esque quality to it, as well as an empty horse paddock that he someday planned to use.

In that northern town winters got dark. There were times, it seemed to me, when the winter weather seemed to animate a person's unsoundness, exacerbate some tiny fissure in their psyche until it took center stage. Sprigg still came and went to work, but his humor was milder, darker and less frequent. Day's burgeoning girth still brought forth Sprigg's comedic lines. Anything made of latex— gloves, catheters, Tonopen covers—inspired comments about the lack of contraception that resulted in Day's unfortunate condition. The Christmas holidays came and went with a baby shower and increasing attention to Day's maternity leave, clinic-wide breast milk paranoia and "baby pool" wagers on her delivery date.

It was January when it happened, about a week before Day had her 9-pound baby boy. Sprigg's schedule had always been erratic. Sometimes he changed things at the last minute and told one person, but the message would fail to disseminate to everyone. Not having him present on a day he was scheduled wasn't extraordinary. But then a second day went by. Then a third. We were in a serious cold slump and a number of people were having trouble with their cars. On the fourth day he missed work, while Jane was scrubbing an anesthetized dog for a spay she asked, nonchalantly "Is Sprigg sick? Is he doing something with semen?"

"I don't know," Day responded, looking at me. I shrugged.

Our office manager walked by, a beefy guy named Shane. "Shane, what's up with Sprigg?"

"Huh?" Shane replied.

The air in the room got colder.

Shane leaned into the surgery area, where Morris was finishing a dog neuter. "Have you heard from Sprigg?"

"No . . . I thought he called *you* . . .".

At that point our communication was reduced to looks of alarm, as we watched Shane pop through the door to reception and ask if anyone had taken a call from Sprigg. Though he'd only missed four workdays, the total time we hadn't heard from him was almost ten days.

"You can't go out there Meghan; you'll go into labor on the way or slip and fall on the ice, or something. One crisis at a time." Morris told Day after she offered to be the one to drive out to check Sprigg's cabin.

"I'll go with Morris when she's done spaying the dog," I indicated the lab puppy Jane was prepping.

"And bring Shane. We might need him."

We drove the 45 minutes to Sprigg's property. What words we exchanged were clipped and practical. It was a moonless, black winter evening, twenty degrees below zero, with ice fog enveloping the few cars on the road, reducing them to a hazy pair of headlights like limbless ghosts. "You ever been out here?" Shane asked Morris, who was clutching a paper with the directions.

"About a year ago. It was summer. I'd never recognize it."

He continued, "I don't know why he wouldn't call . . . I left some messages; maybe the cell reception is bad out here. Maybe he had to visit one of his daughters on emergency."

"It's not that." Morris said.

Fear is given to us for a specific purpose: to keep us safe. The stew of brain chemicals that create the sensation of fear are the ones that make us run from bears, keep our children from playing in traffic, send us to the doctor with an ailment. But our brains have gotten too big; our worlds too complicated. The stress response that helped us when we lived in caves is now capable of creating a reality warped from a fiction.

We finished driving the length of the dirt road and our headlights illuminated Sprigg's Toyota, heavy with frost and clearly not driven in days. No lights came from the cabin. Morris and I got out of Shane's truck almost as soon as he stopped. Shane, slowed by his own fear, lagged behind.

Morris took off her glove to knock on the door and call softly "Victor?" She only called once. Then opened the unlocked door.

The air inside the cabin couldn't have been more than fifty degrees. The wood stove in the middle of the room was silent and dark, not a glow through its little window, not a crackle from within. While Morris moved into the darkness I flicked on the room light. The floor was littered with empty glasses and mugs. Small piles of Kleenex and washcloths were strewn about. A square mirror hung on one of the log walls, but nothing else. An unplugged television set, like a giant black eye, sat in one corner. There, on the couch, curled against four pillows and two wadded up quilts, with a blood-soaked kitchen towel wrapped around one ankle was Sprigg.

"Victor—" Morris said in a tone I'd never heard before, or would hear again, as she fled over to him, pulling one of the quilts up and around his trembling body. "Christ, you have a serious fever~" In response, Sprigg began a coughing fit that tore through his body and infused his pale, greenish cheeks with a sick, red flush. "I'm . . . sss . . . orr . . . y" he tried to speak while his lungs succumbed the spasms and he moved to sit up and lean on Morris. Morris took one of the quilts behind Sprigg and flung it off to the left side of the couch, covering what she and I both saw there.

Shane started "Fuck! Vic, don't be sorry, we . . . ".

Morris shot a quick, knowing glance at me and then looked at Shane. With a tone of calm authority she instructed "Go out and keep the car running. We are going to the hospital." Shane did as he was told, his mouth still open.

Blindly, I found shoes, socks, some kind of overcoat, while Morris mobilized Sprigg. The towel Sprigg had wrapped around his leg had been there for several hours if not days. It fell off to reveal a jagged laceration, oozing and inflamed. It was a dog bite. It would need stitches. En route to the hospital Sprigg alternately mumbled apologies and queries about patients he should've seen that week. He drifted in and out of lucidity, twice jerking straight up in startled horror as if something was again at his ankle.

Sprigg had a life-threatening pneumonia, but recovered completely after two days in the hospital. Once Sprigg was in his warm hospital bed, Morris agreed to be the one to go back to the cabin. She and I had both seen them, the dead bodies of "Maiden" and China". Shane would not have noticed without more time to examine things. In a hurry, they could've been mistaken for clothes or towels. But Morris and I knew what we were looking for. The laceration on Sprigg's leg was from one or both them; he'd shot each of them only once. Sprigg had told us that day at the conference that his greatest fear was being eaten by those dogs. The details seemed so implausible at the time, while the emotional integrity felt abjectly true. His countenance had turned ashen and his voice tremulous in the telling, making us all uncomfortable. It was clear he grappled with the fear of being consumed by revenge.

Once physically recovered, Victor Sprigg had a renewed vigor for everything he did. He traveled more, went on some dates, and eventually left the state to go teach in a veterinary technician program. His first day back after the pneumonia he'd deliberately stuffed a long toilet-paper tail in the back of his pants, just like at the conference when I'd told him of his handicap and he had to spin round and round.

Our monsters take different forms, but none are strangers to any of us. Morris and I never said anything about the dog's' demise. Sprigg never said anything, either.

13

HUMAN RESOURCES

The cow continued her rhythmic chewing with a distant, resigned look in her eye. She was loosely tethered to a banana tree in front of a three-foot-high pile of matooke peelings. The staple food in Uganda, East Africa, is steamed, mashed green bananas. It has the firm taste of calories, of minimally nutritious carbohydrates that gave the lining of your stomach something to make muscle contractions against. The peelings from these bananas have as much food value for a cow as cardboard has for a child.

Holstein dairy cattle, the classic black-and-white cows, had arrived in Uganda in the last few decades. They were a colorful testament to attempts at gentrification of the villages. I knelt in front of my medicine kit a few yards away from where the cow stood. Abraham, my friend and interpreter, spoke Lugandan with the cow's owner. Caramel-colored fecal material ran down the back of the cow's legs even as she continued chewing. I held a bottle of oxytetracyline in my hand. An amber bottle of vitamin supplement leaned against my knee.

"Abraham," I called out. "How much do you think she weighs?"

You could always see Abraham processing before he spoke, not only information, but two (sometimes three) languages, as well as the basic personalities of the people he was working with. This time, however, he was doing math.

"Forty. six. kilos." The annunciation of his English came with an audible 'stop' at the end of each syllable. I stared at him. He was telling me the cow weighed one hundred pounds.

The most striking things about arriving in Uganda were the colors. The soil was blood-red, especially when tracked into the Forex bureau on your shoes after a rain. The trees and the grass were emerald green. The fruits were canary yellow and pink. The citizens had blue-black skin and wore starched, bleached, white shirts and polished, chocolate-colored loafers. Us mzungu ('whitey' both singular and plural) spent many hours commiserating how, regardless of bucket baths and clothing changes, we remained a sweaty, sunburned, rat-haired and dusty bunch. Ugandans didn't even sweat. They kind of *glossed*. And that whole thing about skin color . . . why didn't Europeans get the message to just go-the-fuck-home after that first 16th century blister-pocked burn on their faces?

After three weeks, I knew Abraham's expressions well, and he knew mine. The weight he'd quoted me on the cow was absurd, but he looked certain.

"Are you sure?" I called.

"Well. first. there. is. the. tail. then. there. is. for. the. hoof. and. rib . . . ".

"LIVE weight, Abraham! We're going to try and treat this cow." I called back. I was working in a part of the world where veterinary optimism didn't often pay. Cutting one's losses while there was still time was often the best idea.

"Ah!" He laughed. Our looks of amusement had to be explained in Lugandan to the cow's owner.

I'd traveled to Ndejje village, about forty-five minutes from Uganda's capital, Kampala, to spend six weeks volunteering to teach primary school. Within my first few days, however, I became known as "the mzungu who chases cats; the mzungu who chases chickens; the mzungu who touches dogs" and, my favorite "the mzungu who walks". Ugandans don't go for walks or jogs; their daily lives had more than enough physical activity. I would go for a morning walk and would always end up at a villager's house in front of their livestock pen. I tried to explain that I was a veterinary nurse, not a veterinarian, that I wasn't qualified to actually practice medicine. But there were several realities that worked against me. One: I had the schillings to get into the capitol and buy medications and supplies, the sum of which never cost more than $10.00 USD. Two: that I could read the English printed on the bottles, the formularies and any other Ugandan veterinary resources I could find. And three: there was no one else. I was soon to learn a key tenet of rural East Africa—whatever you could do, you are. There is no more failsafe method of maintaining accountability and quality than to practice a skill in a village setting. At every turn you risk being ostracized or misjudged.

My earliest 'veterinary intervention' came at afternoon teatime. I lived in a compound with a Ugandan family, many orphans, two armed-guards and three other mzungu. Five o'clock came complete with brewed tea and white rolls from a baker down the road who sold goods out of a gutted phonebooth. Joseph, one of our guards, came up to the table with a woman I vaguely recognized.

After listening to the woman, Abraham translated for me. "A. pig. is. down." I shoved my bread roll into my pocket and began walking with the woman down the hill.

We reached a small home that looked like most others in the village: brick walls, dirt floor, metal roofing. Behind the house was a shade-canopy built from banana trees. Inside the coral was an enormous, immobile pig leaning against the poles. Half a dozen children gathered around us.

At first, it appeared the pig couldn't rise, but as soon as I entered the coral she was on her feet and I could see the problem. I walked back to the woman and made a sawing motion in the air between us.

"Kambe?" She asked.

I made the motion of chopping, then stripping the peels off matooke bananas.

"Kambe!" She came back with an enormous knife, shining at its edge. I turned to my patient.

The rope that tethered the animal's back leg to the inside of the coral had gotten hung up so that the pig was literally 'hog-tied'. Pigs are sensitive creatures. Every time I tried to get close enough to handle the rope she grunted and lurched, leaving me prancing about like a clumsy kung-fu fighter. Then I remembered the white roll I had tucked inside my pocket. Back in the States I'd managed to successfully vaccinate almost every breed of puppy using the food-distraction technique.

When I pulled the roll from my pocket and saw the pig begin to respond there was an expressive gasp-like sound from my audience. With the roll as a beacon I backed away until the sow's leg tether was straight and taught. I was emboldened by my audience's rapture. In one fluid motion I dropped the roll, cut the rope at the base of the pig's leg, and stood up, triumphant. But it wasn't genuine admiration on the faces around me, the expressions overall were ones of perplexed distress. As I clambered out of the corral one of the older children pantomimed bringing bread to her mouth, but it wasn't until a small toddler tried to reach towards the empty pocket in my skirt that I realized what had happened. I had solved their pig problem, but I had done it by wasting the food equivalent of foie gras or white truffles. The woman thanked me with an enormous smile and a big hug, saying something to me that I'm sure was a variation of 'don't mind the children'.

Despite the non-medical nature of that house call it only served to spread my name around the village. I continued to teach the elementary children, but I also started making a distressing number of visits to women for whom I could no nothing. The NGO I was working with had tried to start micro-farming projects with the widows in the village, the women left with all the children from extended family members who'd died of AIDS. The organization had chosen pigs. In an ideal situation pigs could farrow almost fourteen piglets. There was a market for the meat, and they didn't need grazing space. But these pigs were only having two or three piglets. They were dying of what many women called 'malaria'. The swine had become burdensome beasts to the women, a gift they felt they could not butcher. Abraham accompanied me to each home to interpret. One day after breakfast in the compound he looked at me. "You. will. not. go. to. school/ You. will. help. the. ladies. For. you. the. knowing. is. important./ We. need. a. plan. for. the. pigs. and. training. the. ladies."

To start my research I did what any American in 2005 would do; I went to the Internet. Kampala city had one Internet café. If you wanted to see white people in any quantity this is where you needed to go. I'd laugh with the other mzungu in the compound as we noted how you never actually saw the white people going to or from the Internet café; they magically appeared there and became lost in the isolating glow of the computer in front of them. To keep your Internet connection going you had to continually return to the fellow at the counter and purchase another half-hour. If you failed to do this at least five minutes before the end of your session the computer would reset itself and erase your history. To top it off, Uganda only had electricity on the days after it rained heavily, due to an extremely dated hydroelectric set-up. This was a problem at the Internet cafe as well as on the street with traffic stop lights.

When I was exhausted from trying to harvest information from the Internet I started walking around Kampala looking for bookstores, looking for textbooks and training manuals. I found a few. They helped a little. They were more expensive than the medications.

It was about this time that Abraham came to me about Peace and Emma Kakande, an older, well-admired couple in the village (many men and boys were called 'Emma', short for Emmanuel) who kept chickens. "They. have. many." Abraham said, before giving me directions to go there. I soon found myself standing in front of a 1,200 square-foot, two-story structure gurgling with a swell of cackling sounds.

"Ahh!" Emma came out from their home to greet me. "You. are. the. veterinary?"

"I am a nurse, yes." He might've been in his sixties, a warm smile and an easy way about him, a slightly more cosmopolitan air than many in the village.

"Our. son. is. at. university. he. will. have. his. credentials. soon. as. well."

"As a veterinarian?" I asked with some trepidation. It would raise the bar on their expectations for me.

"Ah! Yes! But. he. is. in. Nigeria./Come. in. to. our. home. for. tea. and. we. will. talk."

I took one more look at the poultry palace before following him into his home.

Four-hundred chickens. The Kakande's had almost four-hundred chickens, and a rather high percentage were dying off every week. I hauled out the two veterinary books I'd found in Kampala and started my search. I cross-referenced and highlighted and felt like a real Sherlock Holmes, and yet, the closer I got, the more I had to admit the great fist of fear waiting for me at the trailhead to a treatment choice. The Kakande's were clearly important people in this village. And that was a damn lot of birds with which to roll the dice. Finally, I decided on a certain type of water additive that was listed as a treatment for two different possible illnesses. The packets of powder were inexpensive, but it wasn't until I got back to the compound that I broke into a serious sweat over my task. The dilution instructions were in liters. Ugandans carried all their water in tall, yellow plastic jugs. I asked and I asked and I asked, but no one seemed to know exactly how many liters each of the jugs held. I took a deep breath, made a choice about how to instruct Emma, and played confident.

Meanwhile, my pig research had stalled out, specifically around feeding programs for sows. It was fine to know the percentage protein, fiber and fat that each stage of gestation and farrowing required, but I needed to know what was in the actual feed the ladies either had or could easily grow. On one of our walks Abraham had stopped short in front of a macerated field of plants. One woman had dug up all her potatoes before harvest time just to keep her sow alive.

I'd done the Internet and the bookstores. It was time to go to the University of Kampala.

On the outside, the University looked much like any erected after WWII; clusters of concrete buildings, greenspace areas and statues of dead benefactors. I spotted a sign that said "bookstore" and walked in. I expected books and trinkets, snacks and notebooks. One or two of each item were there. Half the shelves were bare.

I finally got to the library and found two armed guards. They looked angry. I had not yet met anyone in Uganda who was angry. My village friends spent lots of time hugging and laughing, trying to make my smile bigger and bigger. "Ah, there . . . now. the. smile. reaches. your. eyes, 'zungu!"

"Foreigner?" one of the guards demanded. I nodded. He pointed me towards an equally grumpy woman behind a desk.

The librarian said it would cost me $50.00 USD to use the library for half-an-hour. That was the average annual wage for a Ugandan for the whole year. Young adult students were everywhere, packed into study kiosks and around tables. They were dressed as if to perform in a symphony, and they were studying as if their lives depended on it. It wasn't until I stepped directly into the narrow ribs of the book stacks that I realized the problem. Idi Amin had gained power in Uganda in 1971. Time had stopped. For libraries, time had gone backwards. Books were defaced and burned. Not a single book on those shelves was dated later than 1968. Some were missing front or back covers. If my library were that wounded and a white American lady tried to enter, I'd charge the crap out of her, too. But where else was I supposed to go for the information I needed? Wasn't a university library supposed to be a bastion of knowledge? It suddenly occurred to me that, like the universities at home, there might be discipline-specific libraries in different buildings. I walked past the angry librarian and out into the sun.

The Department of Animal Science was on the far end of the campus, a modest building sitting on the lip of an expanse of a jade-green hillside. Just inside the building sat a young woman at a table. She had a single book in front of her, nothing else. I greeted her in Lugandan.

"We. speak. English. here," she gently corrected. As succinctly as possible I told her what I needed. "Ah," she said knowingly, "Go. to. room. two. oh. six." A quiet gesture indicated that I was to go up the stairs.

Sunlight streaked the newly-waxed floor of the upstairs hallway. One student, then another, popped out of a doorway to rush off. I arrived in front of door 206. But the sign on the door said "Dr. Philip Muttetika, Head, DAS". I went back downstairs to ask the young woman again.

"No. No. That. is. correct. He. is. the. man. you. need" she assured me. What university department head would talk to me, without an appointment, and without knowing what I needed? It seemed to me there might be more safety in wrestling through books than having to explain the situation to a stranger in charge of an educational institution.

Back upstairs I knocked once, then twice. The door opened. A short Ugandan man, with full cheeks and jovial eyes greeted me "Ah! Welcome!" Had the young woman told him I was arriving? But there was no phone in the room . . . there was no way she could've. "I. am .doctor. Muttetika. What. can. I. help. you. with?"

Dr. M, as I would soon learn to call him, spent more than three hours with me. He'd gotten his education in the States, then returned to Uganda as soon as Idi Amin had left. He had an answer to every question, at one point saying excitedly "I. have. been. waiting. for. a young. person. like. you!" Dr. M took me to an adjacent building to meet Ugandans with the animal health nursing degree that would be comparable to my licensing in the states. We talked about the challenges and direct impediments of certain government agencies, we talked about infrastructure and lack of it. I described getting lost in Kampala while looking for a veterinary clinic. "Ah," he said somberly, "you. have. seen. our. slums." He gave me name after name of people who might talk to me, and where to find them.

It was in the fading afternoon light that I walked back to the taxi park, my mind full as if from an enormous meal. From past experience I was able to reflexively navigate the crush of people in the taxi park to find the specific bus that'd get me back to Ndejje. I stepped aboard the sixteen-passenger van that already held twenty people. Like the first person to call out at a surprise party, Emma Kakande's voice burst forth "Ah! It. is. you!" A moment of panic overtook me. It had been ten days. That's how long it would've taken to kill all their birds if I'd miscalculated their doses.

"It. is. a. success!" Emma yelled ecstatically. Then, to all the passengers around us "This. lady. has. cured. our. chickens!" Someone translated the information for someone else while big smiles erupted with a chorus of congratulatory "Ah!" and "Good!"

I stepped off the matatu at the stop in my village just as the sun was setting. Being exactly on the equator, the sun rose and set at seven a.m. and seven p.m. every day of the year. Sunsets were short and brilliant, a violent fifteen minutes of magenta and orange behind the reaching broadleaf fronds of banana trees. I carried two avocados, three pawpaw fruits, a roll of sweepeps (peppermints), and two AA batteries as gifts from the bus passengers. Emma Kakande paid my taxi fare.

To this day, if I need to remember the basic goodness of people, or remember that the media messages we absorb about foreign countries fail to tell the deep, hopeful truth, I think of Dr. M at the end of our visit. I think of him leaning back in his chair in front of his window that framed cotton clouds suspended in perfect blue above the lush pasture unfurling beyond the campus. "Yes, we. are. poor. And. we. are. rich, too. The. knowledge. and. the. resources . . . it. is. always. inside. the. people."

14

MEDICAL EVIDENCE

radiograph machine company holds an annual contest called "They ate WHAT?" The most absurd image of dietary indiscretion wins a brand-new digital machine. Dogs have eaten cell phones with chargers, dentures, bocce balls (twelve of them), TV remote controls, watches, engagement rings, condoms, rubber alligators and countless pieces of dishtowels. Cats are not so far behind, but their mouths are smaller and, depending on who you ask, they actually do have discretion, unlike dogs. They enjoy swallowing hair ties and sewing needles. For a while they were making the news with a proclivity for a specific type of antidepressant capsule. Someone finally figured out the capsule itself had a fish component. For dogs, we can speculate that the TV remote smelled like greasy prints from pizza rolls or that the cell phone got dropped into a pig pen. But dogs don't eat their own poop because they are lacking something in their diet, they don't eat straw to settle their stomachs, they aren't eating grass for the fond memory of vegetables, they don't eat rocks because they aren't fed enough. Entire graduate study programs are dedicated to finding any kind of evidence for why they do this. We simply don't have it. We have no medical evidence for these self-defeating behaviors.

A few special cases stand out in my memory. From one dog we removed a pair of green panties. As the dog was waking up from surgery we tried to call the man who dropped the dog off but got no answer.

We then tried his wife. She had never owned a green pair of panties. In another case a dog had swallowed an entire 6- to 8-inch-long steak knife. The owner had made the claim, but we were skeptical, until the radiograph came out of the developing solution and my partner could only exclaim "Oh my God!" Such words from the x-ray room were a convocation for others to crowd in. If the offending object hasn't been sitting in the guts for two long, you can watch how the intestines, within mere minutes of freedom, begin their healthy contractions, their pink, moist muscular push of digested food back into the light of day. This means the pet has large puddles of diarrhea on the surgery table and everyone rejoices.

There are some animals, however, with whom something is terribly wrong. They cannot overcome the incredible compulsion to ingest the things that will kill them. I knew a young couple that adopted a black Labrador puppy. They were picture-perfect pet owners. They knew Labradors were high-energy dogs and the husband would to go for bike rides with the dog in a special tether so he could run parallel to his pedaling. They took him to puppy classes and joined the local retriever club to participate in events. When "Licky" (short for Licorice, the owner's niece had named him) was nine months old he ate two rocks, each the size of donut-hole. He bounced back from surgery the way young dogs do, unaffected by any purported sedative effects of pain medication, but no more intelligent.

At fourteen months Licky ate five rocks, of similar shape and size. We unzipped him at the same incision site but cut open the duodenum in a different area to keep the tissue integrity of the small intestine. He recovered again, easily. The owners started putting a basket muzzle on Licky whenever they went camping or on weekend hikes.

At two years of age, in the ten-minute interim between waking in their tent and putting coffee on the campfire—and the muzzle on Licky—he ate two more rocks.

This happened two more times. The owners had invested almost $10,000 in his foreign body surgeries to remove the rocks and had tried every kind of behavioral and physical prohibition. Nothing worked. I clearly remember the day we tried to quiet an exuberant, four-year-old Licky for an intravenous catheter with which to inject his euthanasia solution. Like limp puppets, the owners sat with him for a full hour before they were ready for the doctor to come in and share the final good-bye.

For many years I worked with these cases pragmatically, finding only humor or hassle in their situation. But as I got older, my vision shifted. And by the time I met Ruger, Cherry's dog, I was grappling with larger questions.

Cherry was a Hercules of a woman. Physically she stood 5'10" and was built to move mountains. Her face had a round, porcelain smoothness, her eyes and hair were deep, dark brown. Cherry could use a sewing machine as well as rewire her house for electricity. She mushed teams of sixteen huskies as well as won ballroom dance competitions. She had a quiet assurance about her, an air of having seen the whole pantheon of human behavior before the age of twenty-five. I'd first met Cherry when we worked together at Dr. Vance's clinic. That clinic had a particular hierarchy and no one who hadn't passed the veterinary technician licensure test could do much more that lift, mop, hold, or wash. Cherry hadn't yet taken her exam and was relegated to being exploited for her size to lift heavy objects and reach top shelves. She wasn't more than 23 then. A young man named Carter moved into her life when we were at Vance's clinic. We saw little of Carter, except when he'd come in the back door and meet her in the kennel area to exchange food or house keys. Then came Cherry's pregnancy. We knew about it long before she was showing. One day Cherry was carrying the end of stretcher with a 120-pound dog when doctor Vance backed out of surgery and accidentally bumped into her chest, right at the point of her swelling breasts. "Hey, I'm saving those for the kid!" Cherry objected with a sly smile.

Cherry and Carter got married soon after Petey was born and I went traipsing off on more world travels. We stayed loosely in touch. After some maternity time away from work she found a new clinic, one that honored her skills and paid for her to get her technician license. The day I walked into that new clinic to do relief work (she now would be my supervisor) she blurted, "My kid's in kindergarten, can you believe it?!"

Carter's job had him away from home quite a bit. Cherry alternated sharing standard marital grumblings with sharing no news at all, usually when she was back to living the single life. Petey became part of our lives at the clinic on the days there was no school or he wasn't feeling well. Many of my coworkers had young children and some days the break room was a scattering of books and toys, spilled popcorn and an old TV with a VHS player. Other days the sick little humans would lie on a beanbag chair flushed with fever and making very little commotion.

Enter Ruger. Ruger was a Chihuahua. He wasn't the average ride-in-the-purse small dog with a rhinestone collar. He did not have an attitude of furious entitlement because his feet never touched the ground. Ruger was an actual miniature dog, with the black-brown coloring of a rottweiler, his little feet moving at a great clip, often assuming the 'play bow' and emitting a triumphant bark that was humorous for its lack of acoustic depth. Ruger came to be owned by Cherry when he was left on her porch in a kennel by her aunt. Cherry came into the clinic the following day with the little guy tucked under one arm like a football. All day she called him "*that thing*", as in "I don't know what I'm going to do with *that thing*; I don't know what to feed *that thing*; I think *that thing* actually needs a sweater in the winter."

But Petey adored Ruger; they made barking, laughing pair in the main office if it was winter and out in the fenced back lot if it was warm. The dog and the kid also shared a passion for Legos. Petey exhibited the dedication of a true hobbyist by pouring over catalogs and strategically balancing Christmas requests with those of his birthday and his rewards for the number of stars on his report card. Ruger showed his passion by eating the Legos. I discovered this while I was housesitting for them. Little Ruger trotted out into the snow along with his two, giant, canine housemates and promptly defecated a tiny Lego person with a yellow hard-hat on.

"Yeah, he does that all the time. He especially likes to eat the people. Just close Petey's bedroom door for the week." She told me on the phone. I tried that, but like an addict, he seemed to have Legos stashed all over the house. In reality, it was Petey who was the enabler, leaving Lego pieces behind the couch after they fell off his moon unit when he wheeled them across the headrest. During my ten-day tenure Ruger either defecated or vomited a Lego at least once a day.

To everyone's surprise Ruger's health held out. For quite a while, not a single Lego traveler got hung up in the small or large intestine. Cherry tried everything to corral the Lego debris in the house. Like Licky, however, one minute with their back turned, one minute with Petey's door open while getting ready for school, and the offending objects were on their way to Ruger's stomach. I joked about writing to the company that manufactured Legos and asking what manufacturing chemicals could be so enticing, if any other pets shared Ruger's addiction and, if so, was there a particular color or shape affinity for dogs. In my letter I also planned on asking if they'd make a donation to Ruger's inevitable surgery. It was only a matter of time until the little man with the hard hat wanted to do more than a drive-by through the ileocecal junction.

Week after week, and then many connected months went by while Ruger continually felt compelled to supplement his diet while showing no ill effects. Cherry planned a family vacation to Hawaii and it was time for me to housesit again. Being seasoned skeptics, knowing that at-risk pets (the elderly, the diabetic, the Lego-eaters) either have a crisis or die while under the care of a house sitter, Cherry left enough money with the hospital to cover the cost of a surgery for Ruger in her absence. Everything was set. She sent a text message when they were at the airport at 10 p.m. on Saturday night, saying the dogs were in their kennels and that I should get to the house around 7 a.m. to feed them.

The dogs were happy to see me. Little Ruger spun in circles with excitement, until the door to the yard was open and they bolted outside to pee on things.

I put my laundry in the washing machine. I turned towards the galley kitchen to make coffee when I heard a man clearing his throat.

"Carter!" I reflexively blurted.

"Hey" He grumbled, shuffling into the downstairs bathroom. He had on a dark T-shirt, sweatpants, no socks. I heard the toilet flush and he trundled into the kitchen. "They wouldn't let me on the plane." He paused. He opened the refrigerator and took out a beer. "The police . . .". He didn't finish his sentence but straightened up and let the refrigerator door fall back shut on its own. He seemed to be staring at Petey's Little League photo, affixed by magnets to the upper freezer. He announced. "I was too drunk." A muffled aluminum 'crack' punctuated his words as he went for his first sip of a fresh beer.

After a few seconds I managed to respond. "That can happen." I sounded sage and accepting. I hadn't interacted with him, beyond brief greetings at employee Christmas parties. I knew that he didn't need judgment, advice or hysteria. I was self-centered enough to start calculating how my week would change now that I wasn't housesitting.

He went to the living room and landed heavily on the couch."You know I'm an asshole, don't you?"

I went to the door to let the dogs in. Their busy scurry interrupted my minds spotlight search for the right words, some response that would assuage his self-hate. I wanted to say *I don't think that's true.*

"She didn't tell anyone at work about the treatment centers."

I shut the door but didn't lock it. "No...I don't think she did." Cherry hadn't mentioned anything to me.

"You can still stay here, y'know? I don't wanna be alone all this week."

Scanning my memory, I realized I did have some vague reference points for the Carter I was speaking to that day. On those high volume surgery days I'd occasionally find myself interrupting conversations peppered with words like "drinking", "dumbass" and "seizures". I knew it had been a source of strife, but I never explicitly asked Cherry. But Carter, that day, was a man who was actively terrified of how out-of-control he was. It seeped out of him. There was nothing sexual about his "I don't want to be alone" disclosure, no ulterior motive. The guardrails in his life would be removed for a full ten days if he remained in their house with free time while his family was gone. The reins of accountability had been dropped.

"Could you take a different flight?" I asked. "Catch up with them when you're feeling better?"

He repeated "feeling better" with a bitter chuckle. He was staring off into space as he drank. "She told me to stay the fuck home. I'm an asshole, I told you. I can't fuckin beleive I do this to my family. Petey's patient as hell, but this shit can't go on!" He sprung to his feet and began pacing. The burning energy, the self-hatred, seemed to rumble and amplify with every footfall. It was if he wanted to get something poisonous out of him. He couldn't stop. Then the beer was empty. But there was another one waiting. "But she's a fat bitch. A nagging fat bitch and to hell with the whole thing. She tried to leave once, you know?"

My powers of quick response speech began to slow way down, replaced by a need to observe, study, calculate what to say next. "When?"

"Before second detox last April."

That explained why Cherry had brought the pets to work every day for a full week. It was odd at the time.

The phone in my pocket buzzed with a text message.

"Better get that." Carter said. He knew it would be his wife. He was at the fridge and took out another beer more quickly, without looking at any family pictures or first-grade art this time.

Cherry wrote: *Are you there yet? Carter stayed home. I'm so sorry to get you into this.*

I found I was able to quickly respond to her text: *into what, real life? :)* Only with Carter did I feel mired and slow. The image of small desert lizards entered my mind, camouflaged creatures always aware of flying shadows above, calculating when to scurry or hold still so as not to be detected. Carter's behavior was reminding me of countless others in the past, people I couldn't predict or heal.

Cherry's next text: *Could you get the dogs out and take them to the clinic? I think he won't feed them. You might have to wait until he goes out. He's going to run out of alcohol before the end of the day.*

After I'd agreed and she'd thanked me, I turned my phone off.

"So what'd she write? That I would forget to feed the dogs? I did forget once."

"Yes, she was concerned about that." I was back in the kitchen and had started to make a pot of coffee. Back on the couch, Carter leaned over and let both elbows rest on his knees, face downcast to the carpet, both palms embracing the beer. "What would *you* like me to do with the dogs?" I asked him. The washing machine with my laundry made a chiming sound as the load finished.

"Take 'em. Just take them."

"I have two more loads of laundry...".

"Of course, yeah, finish, stay. Stay as long as you want. I'm just not good alone." He said 'good' the way a kindergarten child would speak of two moral dimensions: good boy or bad boy.

Five hours passed between Carter and me. I was simultaneously aware of every minute and lost to engagement in parts of our conversation. He pulled out his battered and dog-eared copy of the Alcoholics Anonymous blue book as well as his journal from treatment. He read whole sections of his journal to me. We talked about the biology of addiction, sharing the vocabulary of serotonin, dopamine, adrenal collapse, norepinephrine and cerebellum. Yet addiction is one of the few things, it seems to me, that refutes the adage "knowledge is power". More understanding of one's chemical processes doesn't provide relief from suffering. We can redeem this idea that knowledge helps us by stumbling into discussions about how knowledge provides choices, but then we are left discussing whether addiction is a *choice*. If Licky could've understood why he felt compelled to eat rocks, would he have stopped? If the Lego company wrote back to me with insight about why they appeal to Chihuahua dogs could we manipulate Ruger's environment to stop him from the aberrant behavior? For any creature bent on self-harm is external control ever effective? There's a problem with all these questions. To get any further with any of them we have to talk about the spirit and the soul.

Carter spoke to me that day like a man without any skin, revealing enormous personal gore and skipping all small pleasantries. I appreciate that in a person. I require it for a deep friendship. I would not trade those five hours for anything. By noon my laundry was done. Carter was slurring his words. Despite what Cherry had said, he'd stashed plenty of alcohol in the house to get him through several days. On some level he had foreknowledge he wouldn't make the trip with his family. As I packed up, his plea for me to stay and not leave him alone amplified. I doubt I will ever see such desperation in any adult again. Yet, the more he pleaded, the more my desire to escape him escalated. I had to take the dogs, as I'd promised Cherry. I surreptitiously let them out and tucked their supplies into my laundry basket. With much prompting Carter finally got on the phone with someone from AA. As soon as his focus shifted and his back was turned I walked out the door. I loaded the dogs in the car and drove. At the stop sign at the end of the street I realized just how fast my heart was beating. I was that little desert lizard who narrowly missed the diving shadow of and grabbing talons of the hawk.

Cherry continued her vacation and returned. I had a new appreciation for what her 'normal' looked like and how she'd found ways to proceed with life despite what was happening with Carter. It was the week after Cherry returned to work that Ruger finally had trouble with his Lego snacks. As requested, we'd kept her dogs at the clinic and it appeared that Carter had survived his isolation. As soon as Ruger was back in his house, however, like a Hoover vacuum he trolled for lost squares and swords and little men. By Thursday he was vomiting uncontrollably, the liquid brown vomit that smells of feces and misery. He wasn't eating his dog food. He didn't want to play.

All the jokes and ideas about letter writing weren't funny anymore. "Why won't he stop?" Cherry moaned, a fragile quality to her voice I hadn't heard in the ten years I'd known her. "We've tried everything. Petey loves him . . .". I recognized in Cherry what I've experienced myself—a gauzy foreknowledge of the future, a sense that you are on a conveyer belt to a destination against your wish. It's brutal to work as a veterinary technician and face choices about medical treatment and euthanasia in your own pet. You keep thinking there's something more you can do. You're weighed down by your own judgement of your actions, the second-guessing and knowledge of the illimitable ways in which we can keep pets alive. There's always an element of bottled grief as well, an opening of the well of emotion for all the pets we've sent on their way, all our own griefs collapsing to mix with the hearts of the pet owners.

Cherry's feelings moved into tears, which had all of us choking back our own. One of the receptionists offered to keep him in a Lego-free house. "But he eats other things if he can't eat Legos." Cherry explained. Bottle caps, plastic spoons and jewelry were among the things she mentioned. "It's just . . . Legos are his thing, y'know?"

"Yeah, like I eat a whole pint of Ben & Jerry's fudge brownie, resolve never to do it again, then I do it again." Another technician said, trying to lighten the mood.

Cherry opted to euthanize Ruger instead of proceed to surgery. As sick as he was, we'd have to remove a section of intestine.

Unfortunately, that piece of intestine wasn't the cause of his Lego obsession and it wouldn't cure him.

Several months went by. Cherry began to build a new life without Carter; she was nothing if not resilient, resourceful and smart. Divorce proceedings sounded like a nightmare, from what little I understood. I didn't ask, and I don't think it would've helped. On a Monday in May I noticed Cherry had to step away to talk ferociously on her cell phone, an unusual occurrance. One more phone call came through on the clinic's land line which she took, but ended abruptly. At first glance, those of us attending to mundane tasks, thought the men who entered the building at 2 p.m. were from animal control. They were state troopers. It was an energy before it was a reality, it was the knowing before the knowing. I needed something from the doctors' office and turned into the doorway. Cherry was seated. Tears streaked down her flushed face. Four state troopers surrounded her, each slumped into the ache of bad news no one can get used to delivering. Carter had shot himself. He had done a fine, final job of it and it was going to be a real mess to clean up.

I said dumb shit to Cherry in the next few weeks. I ended up being the person who asks *how are you?* Like everyone, you want to make it better, make sense of it, not brick up and wall in a suicide event with the typical taboo. I came to the table with my own baggage, which added to the struggle. The reality is that Cherry knew me well enough by then to forgive me. And Cherry already had everything she needed to go on, she didn't need my bumbling attempts. But she took them anyway, and took them in stride. I sent a text in the first few days after the event. It came from the same place the old broken-kitten dream came from, the one I first had at boarding school. It's a lesson some of us spend our lives learning and forgetting, relearning and forgetting again: *I don't care if this inappropriate to write, but this was supposed to happen. There was no other way, regardless of what you did or didn't do. Turn towards the living. Let them love you.*

interlude: get on the party bus

I worked for Anne and Rachel when they started a full-service veterinary hospital that succeeded beyond their wildest dreams. The two of them became so frenzied with success they could barely maintain their own lives. Rachel came in one morning with two bags of legal paperwork and a grocery bag of food to find her partner already doing a cruciate ligament repair in surgery. "I dreamt about you last night," Rachel said to Anne. "You were doing surgery naked. I think we have the wrong bulbs in those new lights and that's why it gets so hot in there."

"Yes, actually I'm naked under this gown," Anne's words came from behind her surgery mask. "At least you were thinking about me." She joked.

The two of them made a wise choice to regain their freedom by selling to a corporate chain for a tidy sum. Through a business partnership that remained invisible to most of us, the company that now owned our hospital (and owned five other clinics within a 70-mile radius) won the bidding war to take over all the spay and neuter surgeries at the local animal shelter. A sixteen passenger van with the corporate logo showed up in our parking lot one morning. "But have you looked inside the windows?" Another technician asked as we pondered its meaning. "There aren't any seats!" It turned out that a technician would be driving that van to animal control every afternoon to pick up the newly-adopted pets that needed a spay or neuter surgery. They'd be delivered to whichever of the five corporately-owned hospitals in the area was closest to the new owner's residence, where the new pet would have the surgery.

"I'll do it!" I volunteered. Driving around town in the afternoons had appeal. I failed to anticipate I'd need ear plugs, patience, supreme strategic thinking, and a sense of direction (before cell phone GPS). Each afternoon animal control would help me load up carriers that ranged in size from toasters to small apartments as I tried to think through who'd get unloaded first. Don't pack the toy poodle in front of the great dane if the dane was getting dropped off last. Avoid loading the semi-feral cat on top of the barking Labrador pup. Kittens can reach through their kennel's air holes and swipe at other animals. Try, try, try to get the dogs to eliminate before three hours of car time. I can hear, as if it were yesterday, the sound of a hundred-pound saint bernard's powerful urine stream pelting the floor of his plastic carrier. With the same lag time experienced between lightning and thunder, the urine rolled to the front of the cab and pooled under the gas pedal.

The kennels all went back to animal control at the end of the day. At each drop-off site I was responsible for decanting the pets and getting them to a technician in the back. My very last experience being in charge of The Party Bus involved being walked by an enormous boxer puppy. We entered the his drop-off location and he saw an informational poster of a cat, which set him ablaze with joy. He lunged for the poster, tongue lolling, and pulled me right into an unstable display of dry dog food, which promptly imploded with sprays of musketball-shaped kibble. One of the dogs in the waiting room went right for the food as it rolled everywhere. "I'll be damned" the owner remarked, looking up at the receptionist, "he hasn't eaten in three days."

15

MORE THAN THIS

"Are you sure you did it?" Dr. Palmquist asked me. He was holding up a four-pound Yorkshire terrier and wincing as his gloved finger probed the tiny dog's rectum. Fortunately "Sweetie" was still groggy from anesthesia. He continued, "Students have *thought* they'd done it in the past, but they usually just forgot to put the probe cover on."

As a technician intern, one of our jobs on the treatment rotation was to sit with patients recovering from surgery and take rectal temperatures until they were back to normal—about 101°F in the normal dog and cat. While doing so we would sit on padded mats under hot air warming blankets and use every trick in the book not to fall asleep. Our internship days were twelve hours long. Our attention to detail was not primed. I'd put the 4-inch-long probe cover on the end of the thermometer, inserted it into "Sweetie" and removed a thermometer without a probe cover. As an intern you become excellent at one thing: panicking.

"Well, I'm just not feeling it." Dr. Palmquist said, as he pulled the cuff of his rubber glove away from his wrist, over his fingers and off with a finalizing 'snap' sound. He was far calmer than I thought he should be. He was the internal medicine specialist, which automatically made him the default go-to for this kind of issue. "We'll just tell the owner to monitor the stool."

What? I'd not yet seen an exploratory laparotomy, the kind of surgery where you externalize the intestines and witness the incredible length, motility and resiliency even in the tiniest patients. The following week we ended up opening a miniature dachshund who'd feasted on catbox waste. The clumping clay cat litter had swollen and solidified in a long sausage-link arc visible on the radiograph. It took almost four hours of surgery to resect and remove portions of gut. The surgeon used twenty-two suture packets to close the length of the intestines. Within two days of surgery, the dog was almost normal. Though the dog I was then holding in front of Palmquist was only about ten inches long from nose to tail, a four-inch plastic probe cover could easily lounge around in his colon without causing problems.

My internship as a veterinary technician was a reasonable approximation of the trials and terrors experienced by human medical staff in their own training. We arrived at the hospital 4:30 or 5 a.m. with half-eaten granola bars in our pockets and thermoses of coffee. Our bi-weekly reviews in each rotation came with scathing criticism; each reviewer felt it was their turn to give back what had once been given to them. We slept in our cars or went to cry in the low-ceilinged hospital attic. I was fortunate in that the only person ever to find me up there was Dr. Seib, the 6'4" exotic medicine specialist who moonlighted as a stand-up comedian. He'd come in blurry-eyed at 10 a.m. cracking open a root beer. Whenever he bent over a banana or a candy bar would fall out of his lab coat pocket. "Hey girl!" He said to me as I hurried to regain control. "Look at all we did today! We saved that cat and diagnosed those two diabetics! We're a real team, couldn't 'a done it without you!"

Dr. Seib seemed to pay for his virtue of friendliness with concurrent forgetfulness. We had an area at the teaching hospital where the staff could deposit dead animals for us to do the "bagging and tagging". One day Seib left a lizard on the table next to the sink, its name and cremation number already on a manila tag next to its body. The animal slouched, motionless, with a gray-blue pallor to the small spines that ran the length of its body. Yet the angle of the legs was the real giveaway; they were crooked and flexed too many times, the finger-like projections of claws pointed sideways or backwards. Metabolic bone disease in companion reptiles is a common ailment of poor husbandry. These animals need special lighting and a perfect balance of the minerals calcium and phosphorous in their diets to prevent their bones from fracturing. With my cremation bag poised, I picked up the dragon by the tail. It immediately began undulating from side to side in the air, going through the motions of slithering away in the sand if its tail hadn't been caught in my pinch. I shrieked and, of course, dropped it flat on the tile floor whereby it became motionless again, probably from the hundreds of tiny new fractures.

Seib's concerned face appeared in the doorway, "Oh Christ! I forgot I had to euthanize that thing . . . so sorry . . .really . . .".

We went through rotations in surgery, lab, radiology and treatment. Being bumped from one rotation to the next was like being put on stage for a monologue with food in your mouth; you'd barely begun digesting your meal, when a drastically different task was presented to you. But we all wanted to be there. A degree and license as a veterinary technician was our ticket out of waitressing, or to a fresh start in the workforce after raising kids, or a way of gaining respect in our current hospitals, or just something better than shift work at a packing plant. Having watched several good friends graduate from college with general biology degrees and scramble for employment, I'd been dreading the weight of that same mortarboard on my head. I wanted to be able to support myself with meaningful work. I didn't want to be on the interminable treadmill of student loans and delayed gratification while I did those menial jobs. Truth be told, I wasn't a very good student, either, at least not when the immediate relevance of the coursework was opaque.

The Internet was not a widely available research tool at the time, so I went to my public library. I picked out the mammoth *Peterson's Guide to Colleges* and thumbed through the biblically thin pages, inhaling the heady newsprint odor of possibility. Then I found it, a job description listed in one of the indices that I had never heard of but knew should be mine: veterinary technician. The more I read, the more I was ready. I wanted to go to a school that specialized in training vet techs, and I wanted to go there yesterday. I drove 3,000 miles in a two-door Honda with my dog and all my possessions to get my technician degree. Fifteen months later I made the trip in reverse, newly minted and licensed.

The memories of those months in school come up like the montage set to music at the start of a TV series episode. Before the actual internship our classwork kept us in the same large room from 8 a.m. to 5 p.m. without a lunch break beyond the ten minutes before the marathon microbiology class in the afternoon. In order to stay awake I ate Fruit Loops or Life cereal I'd packed in sandwich bags. A classmate who'd brought a single-serve yogurt one day attempted to quietly peel back the foil lid only to have the yogurt burp out onto her face and notepad. Apples and corn chips made too much noise to eat during class lectures. Healthy sandwiches purchased down the road spilled their ingredients with the first bite. We bonded through our need to find quiet, healthy food to get through.

I failed anatomy class the first time (that "no sense of direction" thing again). I resorted to writing the names of muscles, tendons and bones on my limbs with black marker, careful to wear long pants and sweatshirts if forced into public. I wrote an essay about how learning sterile technique was like cultivating faith by going to church. Your surgical behavior was based on belief in the invisible, guided by fear of of an unseen enemy. You would never visually witness bacteria on unwashed hands or unsterilized instruments, yet your lack of respect for such things could cause enormous problems. In surgery anything from the waist down was unclean. The human body, itself, needed to be perceived as a walking disease in order to preserve the purity of the endeavor. I won a small cash award for the essay and used it to stay on the top floor of a fine hotel, looking through the night's darkness into the city and thinking how the clusters of illuminated windows were also like colonies of bacteria. A remake of the movie 101 Dalmatians had been released just long enough before my tenure in school to guarantee that the animal cadavers sent to us by the animal shelter were all Dalmatians. We had to practice cleaning canine teeth by wrenching open the frozen temporomandibular joint until you could hear an audible *crack*. Our anesthesia teacher was a slave-driving beast of a woman who, regardless of the weather or season, wore open-toed shoes and pink polish. She would pace between our aisles of seats and have us chant, "Patients die in recovery! Patients die in recovery! Patients die in recovery!"

I think the sole purpose of going to school may be to scare the shit out of you, regaling you with horror stories about technician incompetence or failure to pay attention: legs falling off because a bandage was too tight, a food slurry accidentally fed into a urinary catheter instead of a feeding tube, the wrong limb amputated because it was written on the whiteboard incorrectly.

While my experience with "Sweetie" and the thermometer probe cover remains the crowning jewel of my treatment rotation, the memory of a dog named "Picnic" hasn't faded. A toast-colored, three-pound Chihuahua, Picnic would stay in the ICU any time his owners were traveling, which was frequently. He arrived with two goose-down pillows and a slice of foam bedding. H also arrived with bottled water and his entire body-weight in dog treats. Picnic's legs had the width and density of number two pencils. His left front leg had fractured two years before while playing with the family's guinea pig. The leg had healed and then broken again, healed and broken. The last time he was left with a housesitter it broke. The last time he was left in the boarding area of the hospital his leg fractured again while on a walk in the exercise area. Picnic's owners paid to keep him in ICU on his pillows where we interns would delicately carry him outside and lower him onto the grass as if putting a diamond ring back on the cushion in the sales display.

Seven of my classmates shared the same rotation schedule as I did, each of us learning a little more about group dynamics and bonding along the way. The hospital was quite famous for the proficiency and frequency with which it performed a back surgery on long-bodied dogs called a hemilaminectomy. It seemed like almost every day we received post-surgical dachshund dogs with a twelve-inch long zipper of sutures along their backs. Occasionally the same surgery was done on a bassett hound or corgi. The hospital had also invested in a therapy swimming pool. Just bigger than a bathtub, the pool had jet-controlled water, against which our patients could swim, but only after we'd secured inflatable arm floats to the upper portion of their stubby legs. Even at their best and brightest, wiener dogs don't enjoy being set adrift in a whirlpool, and we had to underdose their pain medication before physical therapy so they didn't sink. One of my classmates devised a special wetsuit made out of trash can liners that we could wear. Still, at physical therapy time every day interns played rock-paper-scissors for who would "swim the wieners". Always one to keep the peace, I volunteered myself more often than I actually lost the game.

The laboratory rotation was considered an intern's time to relax. Never mind that most mornings started with the lab manager handing you a list of patients, a student partner, and a shower caddy of colored needles and tubes while admonishing you "don't come back until you get those blood samples". Several days began on my knees in the kennel area, hovering under the chin of a rottweiler or other large dog while trying to stab his jugular vein again and again, doing nothing but chasing away the wormy vessel while the dog struggled and my blood pressure boiled until I threw my syringe against the wall behind us.

The lab manager was large. Very large. She didn't walk around the hospital much, usually staying in her swivel chair by her computer with her back to us at the microscopes. Two or three times a day she would interject into our discussions in a way that showed she was still listening, still monitoring. We'd fall back into a tense silence until ear mites, packed red-cell volumes or endocrine tests reminded us to talk about movies we'd seen or food we'd eaten. One day a tiny white puppy, not even a pound, came in to the hospital. It needed bloodwork. You can take no more than 10% of an animal's blood without threatening its life. In horses and saint bernard dogs this is never a problem. Yet a smaller animal, like a budgie bird, has an entire blood volume of one teaspoon. The final image of that lab manager that stays with me is one of a towering, thickened, burnt-out Statue of Liberty, standing in the swarm of the ICU area, one arm thrust into the air with a fluff of pup for a torch while booming to general audience "How much blood can I take from this damn dog?"

Reality television was in its infancy when I was an intern. Our hospital had somehow become the site for a reality show called Emergency Vets. I'd inwardly seethe at the cameramen, with their massive equipment strapped to their bodies, as they walked backwards behind the stretcher I was carrying. Always there, always in the way, they added a layer of self-consciousness to what we did. Several years later, however, I was sitting in the DMV lobby waiting for my number to be called and listlessly watching the television mounted to the wall, when I felt electrocuted. There I was on TV, my head down, hair in my face, pulling a Radio Flyer red wagon with a pot-bellied pig nestled inside. The camera cut to Dr. Seib. "Mr. Snorky comes in every month for a hoof trim, but this time he has a bit of diarrhea . . .".

There are ongoing, heated discussions about what makes a veterinary technician, who has the right to refer to themselves that way, whether on-the-job training should be honored as preparation to take the national exam, and what kind of continuing education should be required to maintain a state license as a veterinary technician. The National Veterinary Technician Exam is required by all states for a professional license. Attending an accredited school as preparation for that exam is not. Many talented, caring individuals have been working in the capacity of veterinary technicians for years without a license, particularly in rural areas. I've had the misfortune to walk into some of these rural clinics and hear from other support staff "You can't come in here with your fancy degree and make more than I do!" I've also been told I never pay attention and always leave the oxygen canister on, bleeding out clinic money and supervisor patience. I've been on top. I've been on the bottom. I've been off to the side. One of the earliest classes required in vet tech school is veterinary terminology, a crash course in the Latin and Greek word salad that attempts to add universality to medical discussions. An ovariohysterectomy is the same thing in the United States, Burma, Djibouti and Zimbabwe, whereas a "spay" is not. In one of these classes the question-answer-discussion time circled back to the licensing of technicians and working alongside unlicensed individuals. The anecdotes dredged up coworker horror stories and how rules, regulations, expectations and pay scales needed to be changed. The class instructor, a small woman in her late thirties, was sitting on the edge of a desk letting the discussion swirl and looking pensive. She finally spoke. "I hear what you are saying, really I do, but licensed or unlicensed, the ugly people eventually weed themselves out. It's not really our job to speed their path."

At midlife, I spend time wondering where our innate character and the time spent inside a vocation intersect. Clearly we are drawn into a work life for many reasons. Is our personality created by what we do, or do we stay in our jobs because of who we are? I excuse myself from veterinary technician positions just long enough to miss them as I would an eye, an ear, a leg, or an arm. With any time spent in the veterinary field technicians seem to either be drawn closer to compassion for people, or further away. Many technicians will vociferously tell you how awful humans are; that they are in the field for the animals. It's difficult to care for people. It can be a real mess.

My internship began at the end of September. Autumn came late year, with its crisp sweet odor harvested from dying leaves. I have all these practical memories of tech school, things that happened or didn't, yet there is literally one moment of memory that punctures the whole experience. Perhaps it was a function of being twenty-three years old, being exhausted, being almost done with school and aching to go home. But in this memory I am the anesthetist on a dog undergoing a three-hour orthopedic surgery. I am sitting at his head, draped off from the action by a curtain of blue. Behind me is an entire pane of glass, the only window in the entire surgery wing. On the other side the November sun squats down and streaks out, like someone scanning a countertop, checking their work for balance and finish. The light is falling onto my record sheet in rose-colored sheaves. I look down at the numbers and circles and arrows undulating on the grid, the blood pressures and breathing and heart rate. A tree outside leans into the wind, and the colored light on my sheet dapples with the shadow. The radio is on softly behind the surgeon's head.

I could feel at the time
There was no way of knowing
Fallen leaves in the night
Who can say where they're blowing
As free as the wind
Hopefully learning
Why the sea on the tide
Has no way of turning

—"More than This" Roxy Music, 1982

16

WHAT HAS BEEN SEEN

Kim Sanders looked like Jennifer Aniston's little sister. Her make-up was fresh, her lips gently glossed with a color one shade darker than nature had given her. Her eyes were hazel, leaning towards a greenish opal, clear and bright, attentive and flickering but not in a nervous way. Her hair was light brown and shiny, sometimes pulled back in a low ponytail with a single strand strategically left out to run the length of her face and swing just below her jawline. She wore khaki pants or tidy jeans, sometimes paired with a t-shirt that was rose-colored, aquamarine, or sunflower—any cheerful color that could be duplicated in nature. Occasionally, in the warm months, she would show up at the hospital in a breezy dress that skimmed her shape, which was perfect and slim. Kim was a client with us while in her late twenties. She disclosed that she was twenty-eight the day she came in for a late-afternoon appointment wearing a corsage pinned to her blouse, explaining that her father had surprised her with an invitation to a birthday dinner-date after she was done.

Kim had a single pet, a black-and-white male cat named Fish.

Once in a great while a cat will be confident enough in a veterinary clinic to act normally, but generally cats are either anxiety extroverts or introverts. Some cats come into the clinic as cage-launching, spitting, screeching beasts (evolution has given them the defense sounds and mechanisms of snakes). Other cats come with all four legs clamped under their bodies, their tails curled in retraction against their haunches, eyes big as marbles, so that they look like fat meatloaves with pointy ears at one end. Presumably this defense mechanism is about making sure the invisible monster mistakes you for a furry rock and doesn't rip off a limb and poke your eyes out. Fish was one of these, a patient stunned into immobility. Kim brought him in annually for his wellness exam and blood screening. From what we knew, they lived in a condo, so his life was devoid of genuine hunting adventures and relegated to crinkle balls and faux mice. There was a scare when he actually ingested the back-half of a mouse toy. But Kim gave him two tablespoons of canned pumpkin (how she did this remains a mystery) to bulk up his stool and found the remains in Fish's catbox not even twenty-four hours later.

In the same way we can classify cats as introverts or extroverts in their hospital behavior, we can say there are two reasons for clients to be immediately forthcoming about what they do for employment. Either they have no money for veterinary care because of XYZ income issues, or they work in a health field and already know the difference between a subcutaneous and intramuscular injection. The vagaries of other client jobs are only revealed after we begin to see their pets consistently. *I work for the university. I do restaurant work. I work for the school district. I'm in construction.* Kim Sanders turned out to be a world-famous limnologist. We only found this out when someone in reception ended up with time to read the Sunday newspaper left over from the weekend. Kim had already completed her Rhodes scholarship in India and was now to travel to East Africa to study the fresh water biology of the area as it pertained to fisheries management, NGOs and public health. We cut out the article and put it in Fish's medical chart.

"My mom took care of Fish last time, while I was in India. She has a house in town, but she practically moved into the condo for four months." Kim smiled. There was a faint air of bashfulness now that we'd discovered the scope of her professional life. "My boyfriend is going to watch him this time." Her face glistened with mischief and triumph as she pronounced the word 'boyfriend', and was quickly followed by a second, more intense dose of bashfulness. "I want to get his exam done and some more of that topical flea and tick stuff just in case. And leave Brian's contact info with you."

We congratulated her on everything. Then we gave terrified little Fishy a pat on the head, dripped the medication on his skin between the shoulder blades per package instructions, and moved on to our more pressing dramas.

It was months later that she came in tanned, and with a sparkler on her finger. It was big. It had a large, square emerald in the middle. She was constantly fidgeting with it, spinning it around or adjusting its base with her thumb. It was a stunning ring, for sure, and we all admired it and congratulated her on her engagement to Brian, but the very presence of the thing on her hand threw off her comportment. And Fish was actually in for a problem this time.

"Do you know when this started?" I asked, rubbing Fish behind the ear to help him relax as I gathered the history for this issue.

"Brian said he noticed it about a week before I got back. It's gotten much worse since I've been home."

"How long has that been?"

"About three weeks. Brian and I are living together now." She flashed another smile.

"And you don't see him scratching? On any parts of his body?"

"No.," she said, perplexed and concerned. "No, nothing."

When Dr. Doran came in I gently ran my hand under Fish's belly and extended his front leg from behind the elbow. Around Fish's wrist was a bald bracelet, about an inch wide all the around the carpus. It was perfectly symmetrical, as if we'd shaved him for a surgery in that area. And it was on the opposite wrist as well, with the very same perfection.

"Huh," Doran expelled a breathy sound as she rolled Fish's paw, and bowed her head to carefully looking underneath, at his paw pads, as if trying to find wads of gum under a table. "No injuries? No paws stuck inside closing cabinets? or chairs tipping over?"

"No . . . nothing . . . " Kim said again.

"No changes in diet or maybe going outside now?"

"No . . . ".

"Well . . ." Doran knew that Kim cared deeply for this cat and, while not of unlimited resources, she was willing to invest more than the average client in diagnostics. Clients like Kim made any vet's job easier, allowing them to answer their scientific curiosity with diagnostic tests. Doran finished "Let's start with some x-rays and a more comprehensive blood panel than the usual. I'll take some hair for a fungal culture."

The fungal culture and radiographs revealed nothing. We were able to run his bloodwork in-hospital nothing was problematic there, either. There was nothing wrong with Fish's little wrists. We gave another dose of the parasiticide we'd given before Kim had left the country and told her what to watch for in case things worsened.

The next person to bring Fish in, almost three weeks later, was Brian. The man was a flat-out jerk. Fortunately he was good looking, with blonde-hair in a very fashionable cut, blue eyes, square jaw, and a faint British accent.

"I don't know what's going on, but this cat doesn't even like me. And I don't much like cats. Kim and her mom have gone all-out Bridezilla on me and had some kind of floral, cake-tasting gig today, so I can't stay if we do more tests. We need to keep the costs down, too."

Fish's naked wrists were indeed no better; they'd actually doubled in width on both wrists. We asked Brian the standard questions we'd already asked Kim. He hadn't the faintest idea how to answer. Doran stroked Fish's denuded forearms which he tried to shyly pull beneath him. "There is something called contact dermatitis. I don't see inflammation here, but have you changed laundry detergents recently? Any change in bedding or where Fish sleeps?"

"Kim does the laundry. I don't know about detergent. The cat sleeps on her side of the bed, sometimes on her pillow. Except when we . . . you know . . .". A smile crept across his face. "It can get pretty loud and then I don't know where the hell he hides."

Doran and I left the room feeling stunned and a bit unclean, each wanting the other to be the one to go back to Brian with the medications. It didn't need to be said, but as I pulled the ointment off the pharmacy shelf and Doran typed notes in the computer she mumbled. "What on earth is the attraction...?"

Kim brought Fish back about ten days later. His wrists were bare up to his elbows, and the exact same type of bald patch was developing on what could be called his bikini area. The patch was a perfect circle with finite edges, about the size of a half-dollar.

"Have you been using the cream?"

"Absolutely, yes!"

"And the steroid dose, is he taking those pills?"

"He takes them in a tiny piece of cheese, exactly as you prescribed. When Brian does it I watch him so I know . . ." Her voice drifted.

". . . that he's actually doing it?" It was another mumbled statement from Doran. Doran was old enough and practiced with heartbreak. Whenever possible she liked to tell young women the truth.

Still holding Fish, I attempted to bring Kim's shining smile back. "When's the wedding?"

My questions backfired. A self-conscious agitation scuttled across Kim's face, and she spun her the ring on her finger. "Well, Brian's brother is going through this nasty divorce that's affecting the whole family, he's taking a leave-of-absence from work to help Tim. They've got to finish the house so it can get sold. so we moved the wedding until next summer. Things should settle down by then. We're thinking maybe run off to Hawaii." Kim did smile for a moment, trying to cheer herself. "And we might be taking care of Brian's dog for a while, a Labrador. That could be pretty fun!"

We agreed Labradors could be fun if you can accommodate their often manic behavior and insatiable appetites.

Doran gave Fish an injection of a broad-spectrum antibiotic and sent his blood to a reference lab to test for endocrine abnormalities.

Fish had no other signs of thyroid or parathyroid trouble, but the lab was thorough and perhaps he had a more esoteric presentation of a common problem. At least it was an action we could take, and it seemed to give Kim some peace-of-mind for the moment.

I was reading a trade publication at lunchtime when I found it. I usually only read the veterinary journals for the pictures, advertisements, or news about weird animal laws trying to get passed in California. But there it was: "Cornell Feline Health Center finds genetic link in fur-mowing anxiety cases. " And there were pictures! Pictures of cats with perfect circles on both haunches, pictures of cats with diamond-shaped baldness on their proximal forelimbs. A certain, small percentage of cats carry the gene for expressing their anxiety by grooming off their hair. My childhood best friend had reflexively plucked out her eyebrows before we started middle school, so it wasn't a cognitive leap for me to understand the behavior in pets. The article went on long enough that it started referring to these cats as simply "mowers", as in, *mowers typically begin exhibiting their anxiety response after the age of two, and often in response to a change in the household.* Brian was a pretty big change in Fish's household.

Doran remarked that she'd heard about mowers in vet school, but hadn't put the whole story together. Now that we had our diagnosis, treatment was simple and inexpensive. Fish needed fluoxetine hydrochloride. Prozac.

One month after we'd started Fish on his kitty anxiety drugs, he came in for a recheck exam. Soft, down-like new fur was coming back in his bald patches. He seemed more confident and slightly less curled up when he arrived at the clinic.

"He's doing so well," started Kim, "even with Tim's dog staying with me!" She scratched Fish under the chin and he half-closed his eyes in pleasure. "It's just like you guys said, Fudge is just this energetic handful, bordering on chaos if he knows there's food around. I've been to that local Labrador club a couple times and even there some members joke it's a support group." She seemed to be forcing herself into the humor of it all. Kim's ring was on her finger, but the question of Brian hung in the room like a noxious fart. Kim looked towards the wall, then towards her feet, finally leaning towards her purse to pull out a piece of gum. I'd never seen her chew gum before. "Brian is out at Tim's for most of the week right now." We all laughed nervously.

"Any trips abroad coming up?" Doran asked.

"I've put off a return to India. I'm polishing up some papers right now, grant writing and Internet work. So, in some ways, it's actually good that Brian is gone for the moment." She chewed her gum and plucked at her ring with her thumb a little more.

We've all been them or known them at some point in our lives: brilliant women felled by their love of a particular asshole; smart, observant women doing everything possible to shield their vision from the singe of romantic reality. The weirdest thing about watching this in Kim was that there didn't seem to be any cracks or fissures in her psyche that would open her to that kind of infection. She seemed maddeningly well-adjusted, so "healthy" that the disruptions in her demeanor since Brian was part of her story embarrassed us.

Not more than three days after we admired the improvement in Fish, Kim called. The receptionist said she'd sounded breathless, distressed, her voice almost shattering. "She said Fudge ate her contact case and lenses and now his eyes were coming out of his head."

Doran, myself, and the two others in the treatment area looked up, utterly perplexed. "She's not herself, I don't think" the receptionist continued. "At least she never seemed like a hysterical person before." Even more than that observation, however, was that Kim had a world-renowned scientific brain that, under normal circumstances, wouldn't have connected dietary indiscretion to eye problems.

They put Kim and Fudge into the "euthanasia room", the one with low lighting, a leather armchair and a fake potted plant. I should've immediately noticed the dog, but Kim's visage grabbed my attention. Her eyes were red and swollen. Her hair was haphazardly bunched into a kind of ponytail-bun, the ends springing out from all directions. She was wearing pajama bottoms with a button-down Oxford shirt that hung down below her hips. The hand that rested on Fudge's head had a naked ring finger.

"I just don't know what . . . ".

Fudge lurched towards me with great Labrador joy, his tail exuberantly wagging, mouth agape and ready for a tennis ball. My hand flew to cover my mouth. Both of Fudge's eyes were about out of their sockets. They were still adhered, so we could be certain he wasn't a zombie dog, but almost 80% of the globe was externalized. He looked like a Looney-Tunes dog that was just handed a plate of T-bone steaks, or—if they made Looney-Tunes expressly for adults—a character that'd just walked in on marital infidelity.

"I can't believe I came in looking like this." Kim pulled at the ends of her untucked shirt and attempted to smooth out a wrinkle in her pajama pants. She looked up at me imploringly, driven to self-disclosure if only to keep herself upright. "Brian left me for Tim's wiii . . ." from behind her hands I heard the faint hiss of the final letter 'f', which, in my opinion, she should've been using to describe Brian.

Whatever was wrong with Fudge, he clearly wasn't dying of it, and, reflexively, I went to Kim's side. When we go to comfort someone in extreme stress we automatically use a different tone in our voices, as if peaceful, deliberate communication will pull the emotions of the person back into the even-tempered world. I was finally able to tell her how much we thought he was an asshole, how almost all of us at some point had been fleeced by love, how it wasn't her fault. This went on for several minutes. From the corner of my eye I registered that Fudge had taken a seat about two feet away. But when I looked up, my hand falling from Kim's shoulder, I noticed that he looked normal. His eyes had completely retracted into their sockets.

"Look Kim . . ." I said, surprised, with hope. She pulled her ruddy, swollen face up from staring at her knees, and the corners of her mouth twitched towards a smile. She reached her hand out to the dog. Fudge came right to her, accepting a scratch behind the ear. "I think I'll keep the damn dog . . ." Then, to Fudge, "Maybe we'll get our own house."

"Did he really eat your contact case?"

"Yeah. We were fighting most of the night. I was throwing things into a bag, not paying attention. I don't know why he did it."

"Labradors eat stuff. It's a mystery."

"I know it's not connected to his eye thing, but I wasn't thinking when I called. Give my apologies to everyone and let's just move on with Fudge."

I took some comfort in the return of her rationality. Then I left to go get Dr. Doran. I prepared her for Kim's state of mind and relayed her request for us to know focus on Fudge and not discuss Brian and her personal life for the moment.

Dr. Doran opened the door on Fudge and he vaulted back into his joy, tail wagging, tongue lolling . . . and eyes popping out of their sockets. Doran's hand also flew to her mouth, just as mine had, as she stifled laughter. Then, she too, took on the smooth tones of someone walking into the middle of a car accident carrying blankets and hot tea. Within minutes Fudge's eyes returned to normal. Doran did a cursory exam "Well, this clearly isn't normal." She said, squatting in front of Fudge and deliberately being as calm as possible so the eyes didn't pop out again. "Doesn't seem to be bothering him... but we don't want his eyes to get stuck that way. "I'm going to go get Dr. Chase to come in and have a look."

Fudge was thrilled when Dr. Chase opened the door. His eyes immediately popped out again. Again, as he calmed, his eyes returned to the safe haven of his sockets. This pattern repeated itself five more times as three doctors and two technicians came into the room out of curiosity only to shake their heads in bafflement.

Doran tried to get on the veterinary networking site but was at a loss as to what search terms would get her to the right discussion boards. We finally brought Fudge back to the extremely exciting treatment area where his eyes promptly popped out and we took a picture. We took a second picture after we'd stroked his ears for a full ten minutes to calm him and send the eyes back to their place. We sent Kim and Fudge home with saline drops for his eyes. "I can use these on my eyes as well?" She joked, her face mildly less flushed.

The pictures, once posted on the networking site, brought forth a response from a famous veterinary ophthalmologist in Denmark. Exophthalmic myositis was a very rare condition in young Labradors and golden retrievers.

Dr. Doran made the phone call to Kim in the treatment area instead of her office.". . . a response from a fellow in Denmark . . . yeah, extremely rare, he asked to contact you with some more questions. He's doing a study . . .". Doran listened. "There's a link from his university to the ophthalmology department if you want to take a look." Doran paused again. "Steroids for one month, high dose then taper off. I've got them up front for you to pick up." Doran listened again, then laughing, "No, you can't take Fish's Prozac." Pause. "Listen, Kim, you need to do some research on freshwater issues in the Scandinavian countries." Pause. "Why? He's good looking." Pause. "No! The ophthalmologist." Pause, then with certainty, "no, he's single. We're looking out for you Kim, really looking out . . .". Pause. "Yeah, I've always been good at puns."

17

NAVIGATION

I was wearing a scrub top and jeans with my "Bel-Rea Institute for Animal Technology" nametag, exactly what my instructor had suggested when he assigned each of us ten hours of volunteer work with large animals. Some of my classmates lined up their hours with cattle, sheep, or swine. I was one of those little girls who papered the walls of her bedroom with magazine cutouts of horses and ponies. I was thrilled at the idea of entering a profession that legitimized my childhood obsession. I was young.

I cupped the velvety-pink nose of the mare in my hand as her breaths came in short, fast puffs, increasing in volume and intensity as the minutes passed. She stood in the narrow stall, blood pouring from the incision site on her side. I had to remind myself how an animal could lose 10% of its blood and how that percentage in a horse would always seem look like an impossible volume. Mare #2438B stared, glassy-eyed into the wall in front of us. She'd had an enormous dose of the tranquilizer ketamine along with smaller quantities of other drugs.

"Doing OK up there? Almost done . . .". To his credit, the surgeon was fast, and not without concern. ". . . if she starts to sway, I need you to slap her on the neck, OK? She *can't* fall down? OK? That would be really bad news for us. OK, almost done!"

As if on queue, my gray mare began to gently list from side-to-side, the slight tremor in her knees becoming a quake.

"Slap her! You won't hurt her!" The surgeon cried.

Her body was drenched in sweat; my slapping had the cracking sound of a child belly-flopping into a pool. I did it again, and again. The surgeon was right, she didn't flinch or change expression. My blows alerted her muscles, and stopped both the swaying and trembling for a few seconds between each of my hits.

Off to the side, behind the surgeon, stood a woman wearing a shimmering gold top made of the silken drapery Tina Turner might wear on stage. She had white cowboy boots and slim fitting jeans. The man with her was also wearing an upscale Western outfit.

"Oh, Todd!" The woman exclaimed while witnessing our blood-soaked procedure. She turned to her partner and buried her head in his shoulder. From where I was standing with the mare I couldn't hear what was said, but I caught the figure of the woman exiting the barn from the door behind her.

The surgeon was nearly done with the last side of his incision. He spoke to the man "We have almost perfected the technique with the bovine insemination wand, but the rates of success with embryo attachment simply aren't the same."

"I read somewhere that the wand is only getting about 30 to 40% success at this point." The man responded.

The surgeon shrugged.

I'd had a chance to look at the zygote under the microscope before the transfer. It shone like a cluster of fat, golden grapes with a sprinkle of sandy potential inside. Earlier in the day "Moonlight Dancer", a fine, muscled, chestnut-colored mare had come in with her tiny kernel of cells still bobbing inside her womb looking for anchorage. Moonlight had been inseminated with sperm from an important stallion six days earlier. She'd come to the Fort Collins, Colorado, Equine Reproduction lab to have the embryo flushed out of her body and placed inside a surrogate mare. The surgeon had outlined a rectangle with black pen on the side of the surrogate, then cut and opened the skin like an oven door. The microscopic horse embryo was placed inside the surrogate where, if it implanted and grew, it would take eleven months to develop into a single, very valuable foal.

The surgeon continued. "We can get higher rates with the wand if you have a really good ultrasonographer on the surrogate. If you can get it down to that twelve-hour window for implantation then rates can go up to 60%. " He paused, drawing back from 2438 B and putting down his scalpel, poking the last knot of suture with one index finger and sighing. "As you can see this isn't that pleasant of a procedure." Then, turning to me "You got it from here? Do you remember where she came from?"

I nodded. He handed me a towel and I ran it along the mare's sides and her neck to dry her off. The stimulus of my rubbing seemed to call her back to her own body; there was more presence in her gaze. I opened the stall door in front of us. She faltered with her first step, but recovered and turned with me as I lead her quietly out the front of the barn.

The Fort Collins equine barn area, when I went to get mare #2438 B, didn't seem complicated. There were a few greenish industrial outbuildings and several clusters of long, white barns arranged to share a courtyard. An occasional wheelbarrow or utility cart loaded with manure and buckets sat, abandoned, as if the operator had been beamed up in the Rapture. But I was bewildered and shaken after watching the embryo transfer, to say nothing of the mare. I was acutely aware of her drugged and dependent trust in my leadership; me, the funny biped animal, weighing less than one-tenth what she did, on the other side of the dirty lead rope, being of the species that had just opened her up to implant another mare's foal. Breeders did this so you could get multiple foals of certain bloodlines within a year, instead of waiting almost an entire year for just one. The expensive mare could then go on with her racing, showing, or other duties without interruption. Mares, like the gray one I was connected to that day, were donated from individuals and organizations.

I walked her down the aisle of one barn, but didn't see the stall with her number. I thought things looked familiar, but then they didn't. The courtyard I popped out into was definitely not familiar. I backtracked, going around behind the building, then inside another barn, to no avail. My mare was slowing. She was tired, Finally, a human being appeared in front of a wheelbarrow. We didn't need an explanation; we *looked* lost.

"That one belongs just over there . . .". He waved me on. Any direction that includes the word "just" is usually not simple.

It felt like "B" and I were truly lost, that we'd never arrive and find rest. When I stopped between barns, all I could feel was the heat of the sun baking through my scrub top. But then there was a breeze, a nice, long, sigh-breath of air from something above that was readying for rain, a breeze that licked through the barnyard. B's face flickered with interest and she whinnied towards the barn on our right. Before her sound was finished, a mare whinnied in return. We'd found it. Settled into her stall next to #5961 A, a sorrel mare with a little square window in her side as well, B drank her portioned water greedily.

At the University of California at Davis they do kidney transplants on cats. You go there with your kitty and get some tests done. Then the doctors find you a matching donor cat from their colony. I've always wanted to visit; I imagine they have a database on each cat, moving down the list until the have the "Aha!" donor match. Maybe the cat has a number. Maybe the people who scoop the cat boxes have a name for her. But, in addition to taking one of her kidneys for your own cat, you take the rest of her home as well, still very much alive.

We can do some amazing things with animals. It's easy to forget that genetic engineering is actually many centuries old. It's called "artificial selection". Its earliest history doesn't include a furrow-browed chemist and a pipette shaped like a jousting lance, but it does include the same level of calculation, record keeping, careful passion and attention to detail. Even after all these years, every time I look at a three-pound Chihuahua in a tiny parka and rhinestone collar I think: this is what we did to wolves. Cats have been a bit more resistant to our manipulations. Even with the Devon rex, sphinx and Persian, all cats are of similar size. In cats, there are only two blood types, while dogs have twenty-three. And, while nearly every female cat can give birth to any male's kittens, the size disparity in dogs makes such free-will dangerous. The frantic owner of a six-pound female yorkie who watched her dog get bred by a fifty-pound elkhound knows that "Princess" will either die by explosion or need an expensive Cesarean section. Mucking about with animal procreation and genetics has created products and outcomes that we want, but generally those with fragility, side effects, and great dependence on human intervention for their care. Floppy-eared dogs get ear infections. Large breed dogs get hip dysplasia and bloat. Schnauzers get pancreatitis and diabetes. Rottweilers get parvovirus and osteosarcoma. But then there are more mysterious illnesses connected to purebred animals, things that just shouldn't happen, or healing that should happen but doesn't, some weird cellular process that refuses to identify itself.

Shar pei dogs are the animals with skin like an extra long tube sock pushed down around a tiny ankle. The same genetic glitch that causes the extra skin and wrinkles in these dogs can be found in humans, but we don't think it's cute and we don't selectively breed to maintain the trait. Most shar pei dogs have a 'horse coat', a type of hair that unilaterally gives technicians a rash on their forearms when we have to restrain these dogs for vaccines or other procedures. They have tiny ears, thick with cartilage like a corn chip. These dogs get terrible ear infections; the inside of the ear looks like the thickened meat of a walnut. They often need the wrinkled skin around their eyes surgically trimmed so their eyelashes don't scrape the cornea. They get yeast infections in their folds and on their feet. And, of course, once inside a veterinary clinic, shar pei dogs are angry. Very angry. Their growling and barking and squealing, however, always has an underwater quality to the noise because of the thickened muzzle.

Like some of their relatives, the chow chow, the akita, and the shiba inu, shar pei dogs are so horribly cute that the need for rabies pole noose restraint or the gives the whole human-animal interaction the air of a macabre love affair. When you meet one of these pets that can handle the stress of the veterinary hospital without getting aggressive, you remember.

It stands to reason that if you're going to pay $1200.00 for a dog, you'd make a similar investment in finding a name for him. Or, perhaps because of some long-winded pedigree name like Zhou Dynasty's Lost Pavilion of the Third Son, this particular family called their dog Wrinkles. Wrinkles was a golden retriever in every way except in physique. As a small pup his exuberance was trapped beneath his pleats of skin. He was so encumbered by his rolls he'd run out of energy. In those first few months his coat retained a downy softness. He finished his vaccine series, came in for his neuter at six months, and then we didn't see him for a while.

"He's vomiting". Wrinkles' owner, a dark-haired woman in her thirties said, as she pinched the back of her toddler's t-shirt to keep him from grabbing the dog biscuit I placed on the floor. I wanted to see if Wrinkles had any interest in eating a treat. To endorse his owner's statement, however, Wrinkles unceremoniously vomited up yellow bile, completely without the gagging fanfare typically exhibited by dogs vomiting.

"It just spills out of him. It's been getting worse over the last five days."

We went through the usual questions. Nothing seemed out of the ordinary. Until I went to take Wrinkles' temperature. It was 106°F.

When we finally took an x-ray of Wrinkles it was difficult to put the pieces together. He'd been shot with a pellet gun, unbeknownst the owner. More times than I can recall, we've taken a pet's x-ray because they're limping on a back leg and found the image of a pellet, sometimes two, in the shoulder or back. These are generally backyard accidents that no one is aware of at the time. But Wrinkles had developed a serious case of peritonitis—an inflammation of the membranous bag that holds all the abdominal organs. While the pellet hadn't passed through anything serious, it was clearly causing Wrinkles trouble. We took him to surgery, emptied his belly of a large amount of fluid, spent an enormous amount of time looking for a tiny pellet, and then placed a feeding tube that would allow us to put medications and nutrition directly into his stomach. He was a young dog, the prognosis was good.

The first day after surgery Wrinkles seemed to feel quite well. We could place medication through the tube and into his stomach to prevent him from vomiting and then feed him small amounts. His family came to visit. Our wrinkled friend wagged his funny-looking tail.

I was first to arrive the following morning and went to Wrinkles' kennel to start his medications. You know that feeling of being so stunned you can't move, while your brain tries to make sense of what is happening? Despite myself, I laughed. I was overcome with pity as Wrinkles tried to wag his tail for me. Somehow—and the only possible way would've been because of the feeding tube—Wrinkles had "inflated" overnight. The medical term is subcutaneous emphysema (air underneath the skin). Wrinkles looked like a Zeppelin. If you went to pat him on the side he sounded like a ripe watermelon: thump, thump. Beyond preventative antibiotics and his other medications for vomiting, there wasn't a medication that would address such a problem. At the direction of the doctor we made a compression bandage. The bandage covered everything but Wrinkles' lower limbs and the very front of his face, the eyes and nose. The pressure of the wrap pushed his inflation up behind his ears so that his face looked like that of a marshmallow lion. He was such an endearing, wonderful sport about it, completely unaware of the comic relief he was generating.

Wrinkles stayed with us for two weeks. In that period of time we medicated him with absolutely everything to stop the vomiting. His inflation problem resolved within a few days through the help of maudlin renditions of flatulence and belching, but the pernicious problem with his intestines did not relent. We put medications into his tube at specifically timed intervals before feeding him the minute amounts. We preceded those medications with injections. We attempted to control absolutely every variable to help him heal. His two-week hospital stay was an astronomical fee for his family. We euthanized Wrinkles on December 24 in front of his family.

The story about Wrinkles isn't meant to indict dog breeders. Animals that have been genetically modified have a special place within human care and concern. What we can say about our ability to manipulate nature is that for every "solution" we create a problem. It may be biological, ethical or moral, but it's always there.

Around the time I did my volunteer work with the horses in Colorado, the first cloned animal hit the news: Dolly the sheep. Then there was the "Missyplicity Project" that attempted to clone "Missy" the dog. Like a 1950's Sci-Fi novel come to life, an elderly financier founded "Genetics Savings & Clone" aspiring to help grieving pet owners recreate their loved one, to, in effect, better align the lifespan of humans with the longevity of a beloved animal.

On February 14, 2002 Texas A&M University unveiled a photo of an 8-week-old kitten sitting inside a glass beaker. This was the world's first cloned pet, named "CC" for copycat, a healthy, round little creature with a final surprise for Genetics Savings & Clone. She was a different color than her original. CC was a perfect clone of a calico cat named "Rainbow", but CC was tabby and white. What happened is not a complete mystery. If an animal's genetic code is an old-fashioned telephone switchboard, it still requires an operator to turn things off and on at certain times. As of this writing, CC is a healthy adult cat, slightly overweight, sprawled in some patch of sunlight, and unaware of her place in our scientific expectations. She is proof that some things do only come to us once. Genetics Savings & Clone disbanded in 2006.

Because we are human we can't stay away from manipulating the world around us. We must continue to prove our power to ourselves or we get bored. We blast through mountains and rearrange telomeres.

Unlike the biblical story of creation, we never find our day of rest. From space we look at earth as if she were a marble; from a single cell we can see unlimited potential. Because we are human we will continue to look down the taunting barrels of microscopes and think we can improve on what we've been given. But there are moments when we reach an impasse, when something is understood but still not under our control, when our best attempts yield only mystery. Something else exists as the protectorate. It's the hand that will not loosen its grip on the contents of the soul, nor reveal to any scientist the full meaning of life. That hand will beckon to us, but it will not let us lose our way.